DUOTONE

HOAKI

HOAKI

Hoaki Books, S.L.
C/ Ausiàs March, 128
08013 Barcelona, Spain
T. 0034 935 952 283
F. 0034 932 654 883
info@hoaki.com
www.hoaki.com

hoaki_books

Duotone
Limited Colour Scheme in Graphic Design

ISBN: 978-84-17656-53-9

Second edition 2022

Copyright © 2022 Hoaki Books, S.L.
Copyright © 2018 Sandu Publishing Co. Ltd.

Sponsored by Design 360°
– Concept and Design Magazine
Edited, produced, book design, concepts & art direction by
Sandu Publishing Co., Ltd.
info@sandupublishing.com
Editor: Design 360° Magazine

D.L.: B 18961-2021
Printed in Turkey

CONTENTS

182 Gradation

233 Index

240 Acknowledgements

Preface

by Shanti Sparrow

Colour is possibly the most powerful design element. It has the capacity to affect the meaning, tone, and emotion of a design. Colour is a useful psychological tool that has the ability to deeply influence an audience. With a toggle of a hue slider, we can create serenity in a harmonious monotone scheme or cause discomfort through the use of a jarring complementary pairing.

Choosing effective colours within a design is a collaboration of art, experience, and science. This is because colour is both highly subjective and highly technical. Subconsciously, we react to the colours that we learned in childhood. We associate red with danger, heat, and warning, while greens evoke a sense of growth and nature. Colour communicates meaning, and so we need to be conscious of what message we're conveying when we choose to use one colour over another. Technically speaking, there are seemingly endless ways to classify and sort colours: cool, warm, hot, cold, neutral, primary, secondary, tertiary, tints, shades, and tones, to name just a few. Cultural differences can compound these associations; a hue that's passionate and seductive in one country may be interpreted as mournful and somber in another. It is our job as designers to be informed about these connotations and craft considered and appropriate palettes.

With this great power comes great responsibility. Unbridled colour use can result in an unfocused aesthetic. The more colours you use, the harder it can be to use them effectively. Too many colours competing for attention can cause hierarchies and focal points to be lost.

In my practice as a designer, I worship colour. I relish creating vibrant, confident brands filled with neons, pastels and high contrast. My process always starts with the brief, and specifically in the form of focusing on emotive keywords.

Does the client wish to appear raw, serene, and holistic, or do they wish to appear powerful, bold, and confident? These key words lead me to applicable colour possibilities that communicate the client's intention. I research the client's competitors and often choose to use a colour palette that will help differentiate them visually within their industry. Additional historical research may provide insight into colours that should be either embraced or avoided. I generally construct a palette with a maximum of four colours, including a neutral one. This is a flexible and workable number that provides both variety and control. This rule of thumb, however, is not always the best option. Some of my most dramatic and recognizable works use only one or two colours. Having the confidence to use a limited palette is a bold choice and can certainly have a big visual impact.

When colour options appear endless, it is often strategically advisable to constrain yourself to a two-colour system. Limiting colours, however, does not limit creativity. Within these confines, you can express a wide range of emotions. You can run the gamut of pairing possibilities, from vibrant clashing neons to sympathetic neutral pastels.

I look for inspiration on limited palettes in the Swiss masters who created the International Typographic Style. They embraced a minimalistic use of graphic elements and colour as well as high-contrast colour pairings, which have resulted in work that has stood the test of time. Swiss style is unarguably iconic, and minimalist philosophy continues to inspire new generations of designers.

Duotone creates a more distinctive and recognizable visual relationship within a brand identity. This aesthetic repetition is especially effective when viewed in a dynamic system with multiple touch points. This is evident across both digital and print platforms. A great example of this is seen within event branding. Everything from the website to tickets, merchandise, posters, advertising, and signage is strongly tied together, primarily through the strategic use of colour.

Another benefit of duotone is that the technique creates practical negative space. Selecting low-contrasting colour sets allows the image to be utilized as a background. This often provides space for key typography and supporting content. As a bonus, duotone can also be a more cost-effective printing technique, as it uses less ink. This can be a clever way to navigate between budget and ambition.

Using duotone on images removes the reality of the photograph and allows the designer to put it into new context. An image treated in complex earthy tones has a wildly different meaning to the same image when it is treated in bright pop colours. Colour choice changes the way in which illustration, typography, and photography are interpreted. Even a subtle variation in the hue or saturation of a colour can evoke a completely different feeling.

This volume is a collection of some of the most inspirational examples of limited colour use. I love the power and possibility of colour and am encouraged to see continual innovations and adaptability in its use. From large-scale visual identities to bespoke handmade zines, each work showcases the impact of duotone and limited colour. This book provides evidence that restrained colour application creates truly iconic and memorable designs.

●

When colour options appear endless,
it is often strategically advisable to
constrain yourself to a two-colour system.
Limiting colours, however, does not
limit creativity.

●

Colour Matching

1+1=2

PANTONE Reflex Blue C+
PANTONE 032 C

State of the Art

Design Studio: Studio Lennarts & de Bruijn
Client: Royal Academy of Art, The Hague

For the annually open day of Royal Academy of Art, The Hague (KABK), Studio Lennarts & de Bruijn created the campaign based around the idea of it being a community and its internationality. They decided to call it "The State of The Art", as a play on words but also to raise the question if a state can still exist. During this day and age, where are the boundaries? And when are you a local? They tried to use multiple sides of the saying in the visuals. State as a location, flags, colours, wording, drummers, clothing, etc, and as a state of time, 360 cameras, coding and 3d rendering.

WISHING YOU DOUBLE RAINBOWS!!

ROYAL ACADEMY OF ART THE HAGUE
WWW.KABK.NL

NE 1ST

THE STATE OF THE ART
SINCE 1682

KABK.NL

SATURDAY
23 JAN.2016
10:00 – 16:00

SPECTACULAR VIEWS

OPEN DAY!!!!

ROYAL ACADEMY OF ART

THE HAGUE

ROYAL ACADEMY OF ART THE HAGUE

OPEN DAY!!

SATURDAY
23 JAN 2016
10:00 – 16:00

WWW.KABK.NL

GET HIGH ON RESEARCH

THE STATE OF THE ART
SINCE 1682

ROYAL ACADEMY OF ART THE HAGUE

C0 M83 Y73 K0 + C99 M100 Y0 K19

CTD'A

Design Studio: Gauthier
Creative Directors: Shawn Bedford, Lisa Tremblay
Designer: Alix Neyvoz
Photographer: Christian Blais
Client: Centre du Théâtre d'Aujourd'hui

Hero or anti-hero? During the 2017/18 season of the Centre du Théâtre d'Aujourd'hui, the authors raised interesting questions. Campaign imagery was based on actors in character, represented visually as cartoon-like icons. They stand alone or in groups, resisting and questioning each other. The portraits were set on red or white backgrounds, coupled with bold lettering, reminding viewers of posters depicting major social movements.

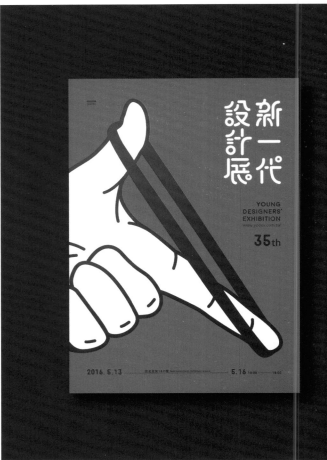

 PANTONE Bright Red C + PANTONE 2368 C

Generation Q:
2016 YODEX Proposal

Art Directors: Szu-Wei Cheng, Sheng-Hsiung Yang, Page Tsou
Creative Director/Team Leader: Verena Hsieh
Designers: Verena Hsieh, Zora Wu, Karen Chang, Sharmaine Liu
Client: Taiwan Design Center

Through this project, the group of young designers, who are born after the 1990s, declare to the public that they are the Generation Q: Quick! Queer! Questions!

Red stands for the passion and energy of the YODEX designers. Blue symbolizes that this generation has to stay calm and to assess before reaching a conclusion under the age of information explosion. The cool and warm colours mingle together designers' reason and feelings, bringing out the unprecedented aesthetics.

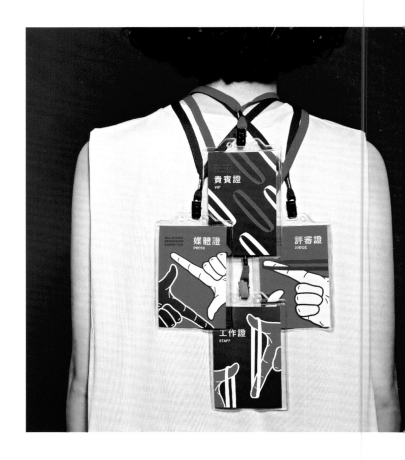

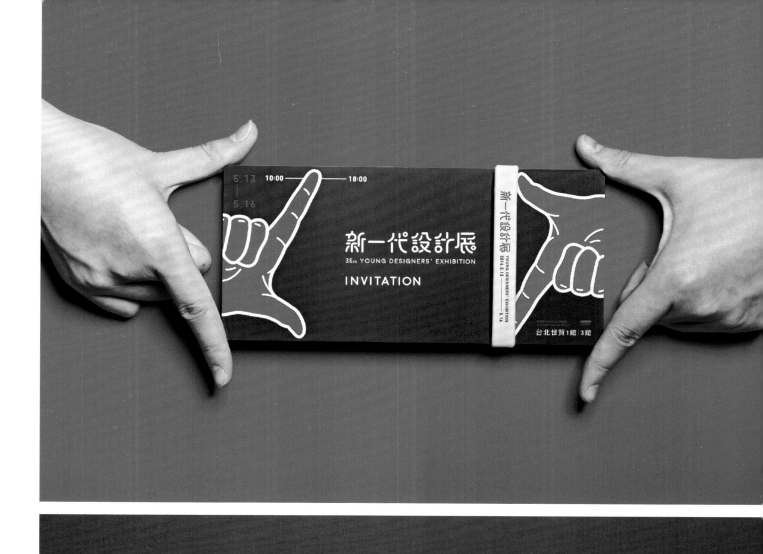
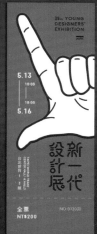

Risograph Ink: Bright Red + Medium Blue

Baraja Española

Designer: Laura Cárdenas

Inspired by her grandparents who play every night with the Spanish deck, the designer decided to redesign the traditional Spanish pack of cards. This new, simple, clear and modern design changes the way that old and new generations see and play with the cards. The deck consists of 50 cards, printed in bright red and medium blue with Risograph print. They are perfect for playing, Tarot readings, witchcraft, collecting or just good gifts for friends.

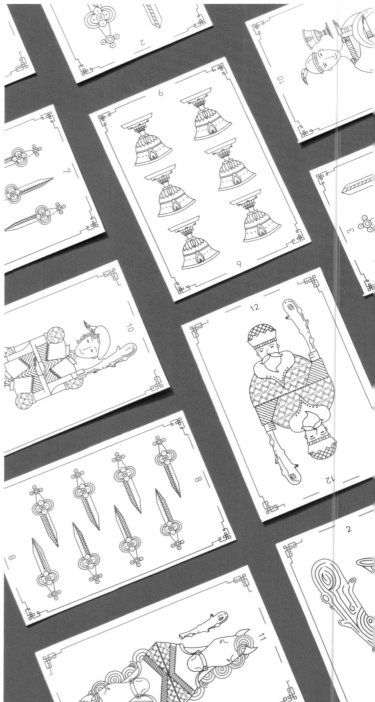

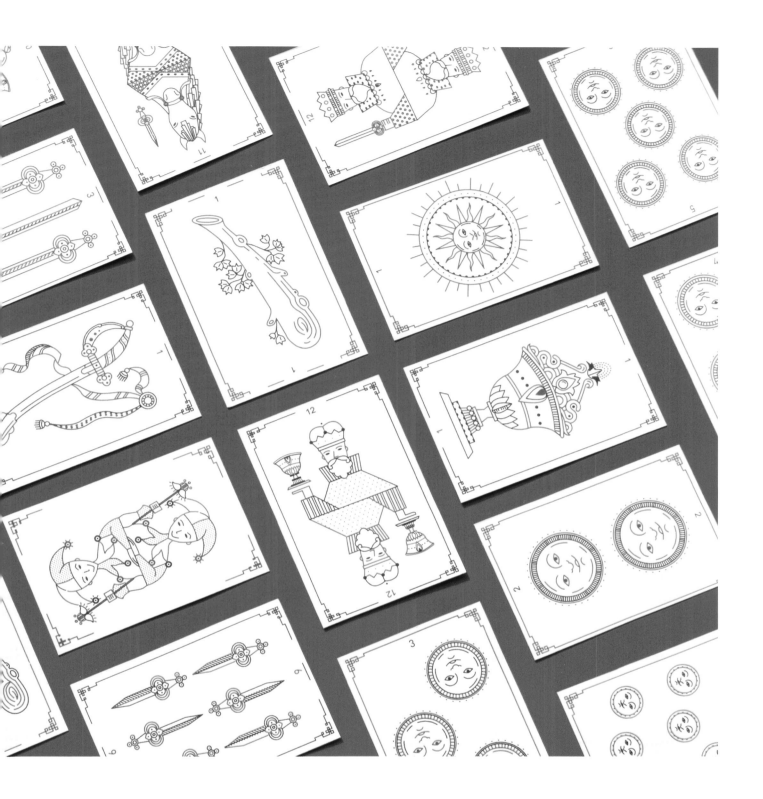

 #EB4970 + #31338C

This Is Lincoln Calling

Design Studio: Justin Kemerling Design Co.
Designer: Justin Kemerling
Client: Hear Nebraska

This approach to Lincoln Calling, a music festival in its 13th year, was to remove any specific reference to place, either with buildings, landscapes, or historical figures. With only a subtle Clash reference in the name itself, the designer wanted to instead design for the sonic storm cloud that the festival ultimately is. A loud, epic thunder crash, the music event of the Midwest. He wanted the duotone palette to battle it out as each individual colour sought dominance over the other in a colossal back and forth of aesthetic tug of war, calling out from the Great Plains, striking colour, in an atmospheric assembly of eruption and spectacle. Hear Nebraska is a nonprofit organization who ran the event. They meaningfully connect and engage fans, artists, and communities through music journalism, education, and events.

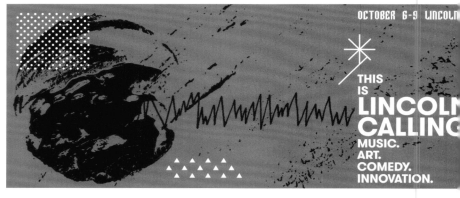

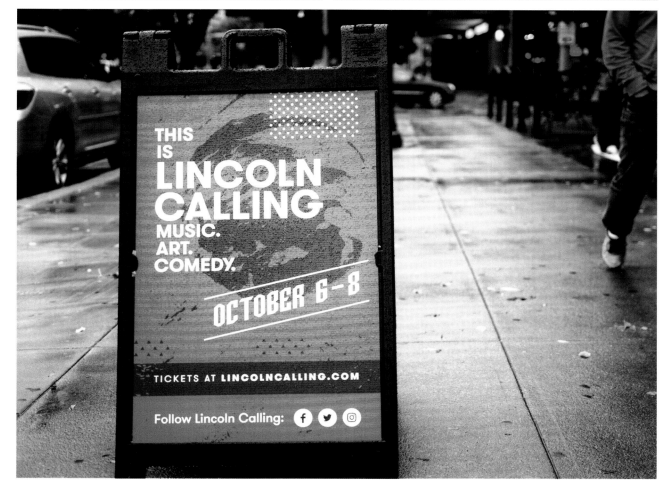

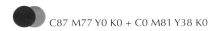

C87 M77 Y0 K0 + C0 M81 Y38 K0

Aborígens

Design Studio: Toormix
Client: Aborígens · Local Food Insiders

Branding and corporate materials for Aborígens, a gastronomic consultancy in Barcelona aimed at professionals in the food, hotel and catering industry, that also makes its knowledge available to visitors of the city through gastronomic tours.

The casual identity seeks to align the tone of proximity of Aborígens with the customer through a humorous tone, placing the company in the gastronomic sector and communicating the climate that the team generates in their tours and projects. The design studio Toormix selected funny and decadent images from Google images, as well as pictures of cats, which the team members imitated in a fun way, to offer an exaggerated nod to the tours and their consequences.

1 Degree // 2 Degrees

Designer: Belen Ramos
Client: Remi Roehrs

1 Degree // 2 Degrees was a two-part exhibition series surveying the work of, and connections between, Brisbane's female artists, creatives and designers. Belen was commissioned to create the branding for the event. At 1 Degree, all artists were within one degree of separation from the curator, whilst at 2 Degrees each participant was in charge of nominating a female artist or creative. The goal was to create an outwards-reaching network of creativity and empowerment for Brisbane's female artists. The branding explores this idea of connectivity through a pattern of lines and dots which was inspired by the childhood game "connect the dots". On the other hand, the imagery celebrates women, whilst also explores the way women have been portrayed in the past—whether in art, photography, or illustration. The colour palette utilises red and blue, colours that are strongly associated to both men and women. Red also tends to represent passion, while blue conveys knowledge and power, characteristics of the female involved in this exhibition.

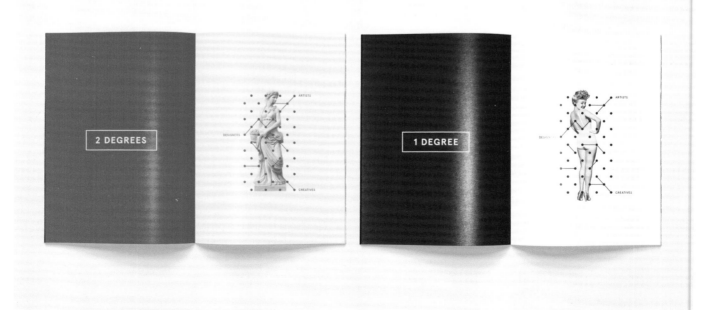

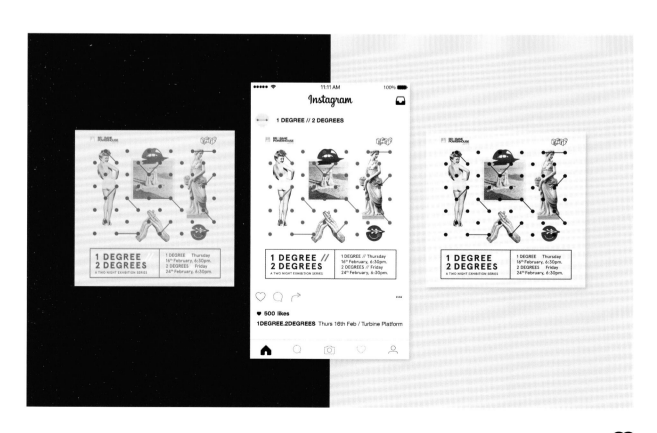

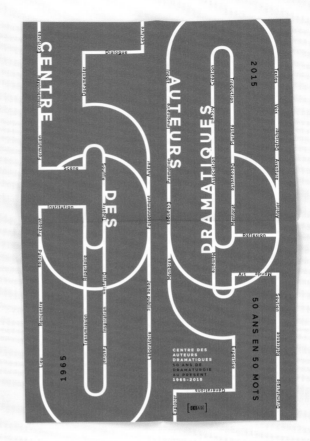

PANTONE 185 U + PANTONE 280 U

Les 50 ans du CEAD

Design Studio: Le Séisme
Creative Director: Maxime David
Designer: Maxime David
Client: Centre des auteurs dramatiques (CEAD)

The Centre des auteurs dramatiques is a center of support, promotion and distribution of French-language dramaturgy in Quebec and Canada. Located in Montréal, the CEAD turned 50 in 2015. To celebrate the organization and to provide more information about its mission, Le Séisme made a special leaflet. The concept was to play with the number 50 and a list of 50 words related to the organization.

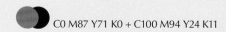 C0 M87 Y71 K0 + C100 M94 Y24 K11

Snapshot Poster

Design Studio: Blind
Creative Director: Chris Do
Designer: Minhye Cho
Client: The Futur

Snapshot is a show segment for the Futur's Youtube Channel, which offers audiences the ability to peek behind the scenes. The visuals were inspired by the look of traditional image making—camera, film negative, and proof sheets. These were then deconstructed and reassembled for the poster concept; a byproduct of the main title sequence. The designers chose two colours that were different on the colour spectrum (warm/cool) but had equal visual weight.

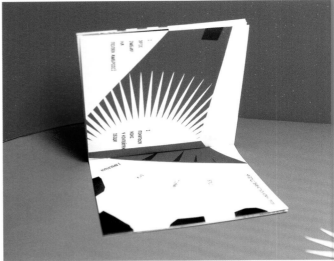

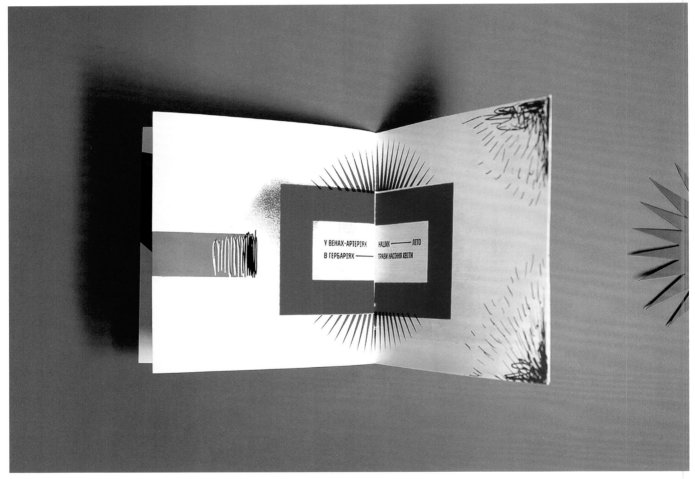

 Printed by hand in silk-screen printing
C0 M100 Y100 K0+ C76 M24 Y0 K0

Fanzine "Inhalation"

Designer: Mary Vinogradova
Client: KSADA

Fanzine "Inhalation", pinted by hand in silk-screen printing, is inspired by one of the poem of Ukrainian writer and poet, Yuri Izdryk. The main theme of the poem was expressed in the form of two similar barbed suns that exist in opposition to each other, like good and evil, and is associated with the dualism of the world. Several sharp geometric shapes, free layout, use of blue and red colours—all support the inner tension of the poem. Blue and red, two powerful colours that create a new one when mixed, but here they are represented in the fight, like two different poles, warm and cold, plus and minus.

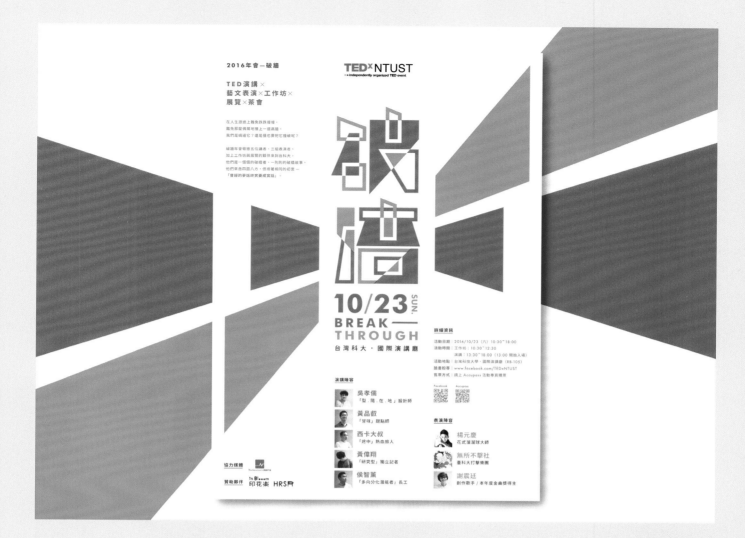

 R239 G67 B38 + R0 G179 B240

TEDxNTUST 2016 – Breakthrough

Designer: Chiun Hau You
Client: TEDxNTUST

"Breakthrough" is the main theme of the TEDxNTUST 2016, which encourages young adults to think outside the box and make innovation. The designer Chiun Hau You used quadrangles to compose the whole branding with only two colours, red and blue, to maintain simplicity and achieve the feeling of firm and persistent.

 R255 G93 B85 + R63 G92 B170

Our Renaissance – TEDxNTUST 2017 Event Identity

Designer: Chiun Hau You
Client: TEDxNTUST

With the theme "listening to the river", the designer Chiun Hau You wrote a JavaScript program to generate the river-like flow graphic. He used blue and red to achieve an image of ocean, river and sunset, and to strike a balance between cold and hot.

  #63BCA0 + #2B4E9D   Paper Colour: #FF5A5F

THE

Designer: Michelangelo Greco

Michelangelo Greco was asked to create a personal profile of the unknown subject. Having no idea who the subject was, the designer made a journey to understand the subject and created his vision. He perceived a subject linked to the Punk / Grunge language, fundamentally rabid and inculcating in the "no future". To accomplish his journey, he has used the instrument of magnification and decontextualization, reconnecting to some elements that characterized the graphics typical of the punk period.

Starting from the definite article extrapolated from every speech, he conducted in the first part an experimentation with typography playing with zooming(age/rage), overlaps and metalanguage to visualize the concept through the word that expresses the same(Machine). In the second part, he tried to reconstruct the unknown subject with pure graphic experimentation playing with negative spaces, shapes and subjects. The whole is connected by a general exaggeration in full punk spirit, and by the use of the bitmap, colour method that excludes any halftone that resembles the strong contrast of grunge.

 C12 M95 Y89 K2 + C92 M75 Y0 K0

Recital Poster

Design Studio: Acrobat Wisefull
Creative Director: Robert Bąk
Designer: Justyna Radziej
Client: Academic Choir University of Gdansk

Recital Poster refers to a dualistic arrangement of playing cards, which depict two different events and two different debut concerts of soloists from Academic Choir University of Gdansk. The team from University of Gdansk is one of the most appreciated choirs in Poland. Since the establishment in 1971, the Choir has given numerous concerts in the country and abroad.

 #CD1F35 + #252772

Good Luck to Chinese New Year Celebrate Package – The Year of Dog

Creative Directors: WANG2MU, Supersonic
Designers: WANG2MU, Supersonic
Client: ADQUAN.COM

It has been a while that Chinese advertising practitioners call themselves as "advertising dog", a phrase of self-mockery, which means they constantly have to ingratiate themselves with their clients and work day and night. At the beginning of "The Year of Dog" in China, independent designer WANG2MU collaborated with the media platform ADQUAN.COM to present this lucky gift – New Year Celebrate Package. The character of dog and traditional Chinese New Year elements are merged with the key issues concerned by advertising practitioners, such as successfully receiving the payment and creating a popular article. The Package contains sincere wish that practitioners in communication and creative industry could have a good start of the year.

C15 M98 Y100 K5 +
C85 M77 Y33 K20

Satay Brothers: Menu Monsters

Design Studio: Les Évadés
Creative Director: Charles Gagnon
Art Director: Martin Dupuis
Illustrator: Cristian Robles
Silkscreen Printing: La Bourgeoise Sérigraphe
Client: Satay Brothers

The idea behind the posters was to make monsters out of food items from the Satay Brothers restaurant. The illustrator was given reference images from their menu (soup, sandwich, tofu, noodles, beef, chicken satay sticks) and created the creatures from it all.

Looming behind the overall concept are references taken from Godzilla towering over unsuspecting crowds to old Japanese folk tales of "Hungry Ghosts" (cursed spirits with an insatiable hunger for a particular substance or object). Together with the illustrator, the design team crafted and refined all the small details to project the right array of reactions from the customers: some run scared, some are playful while others are completely unfazed by the craziness and just keep eating.

The red and blue duotone palette was used to mimic the traditional Chinese colours often seen on plates and decor. Only having two colours allowed the image to have a clear-cut division between the main creatures and their dense backgrounds. Its duotone process also allowed the piece to be printed as hand made silkscreens.

SATAY BROTHERS

SOUTHEAST ASIAN SPECIALTIES

 PANTONE Warm Red C +
PANTONE Blue 027

YunTech VCD
Graduation Market

Designer: Fast, Liang
Client: Yuntech VCD Graduation Market

Yuntech Visual Communication Design (VCD) graduation market, a flea market that lasted for three days, was organized by recent graduates of VCD department.

The visual identity was comprised of three graphics, the trencher cap, the icon of the eye which represents VCD, and a pair of loud speakers, which clearly convey the information and recreate the lively atmosphere. For the colour system, the designer chose complimentary colours. Red stands for the energetic and spirited characteristic of young adults, while blue calls for reflection. The use of red and blue also represent the balance of sensibility and rationality in making design.

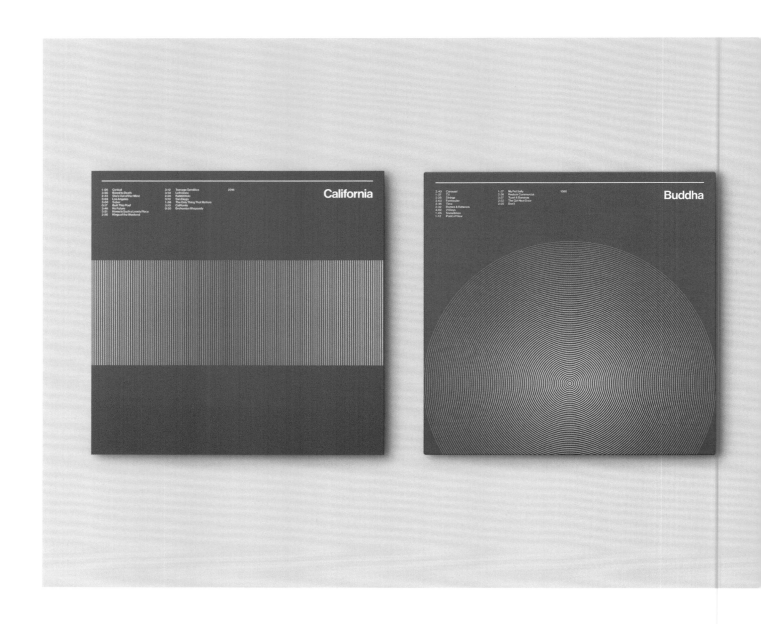

From left to right

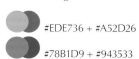 #EDE736 + #A52D26

 #EDE736 + #626E97

#78B1D9 + #943533

#A52D26 + #262425

Blink182 Album Covers

Designer: Brandon Fretwell

"Blink182" is the redesign of the visual branding for a band/artist discography. For this project, the designer Brandon Fretwell wanted to bring music and design together. He chose the band "Blink 182" because of his long history listening to them and with the release of California, the band's seventh studio album since 2011, he felt this was a great opportunity to redesign all of the albums together and really explore their music and artistic identity to commemorate their successful career in the form of a vinyl box set. Before online streaming, bands were remembered by the iconic artwork found on the albums they released. Building upon this idea, Brandon decided to redesign all of their seven album covers so that each of them would highlight key design elements found in each artwork, and unifying the design with basic shapes and colour palette found within the original covers.

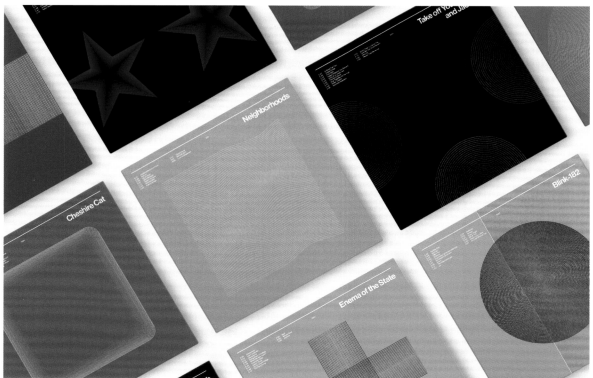

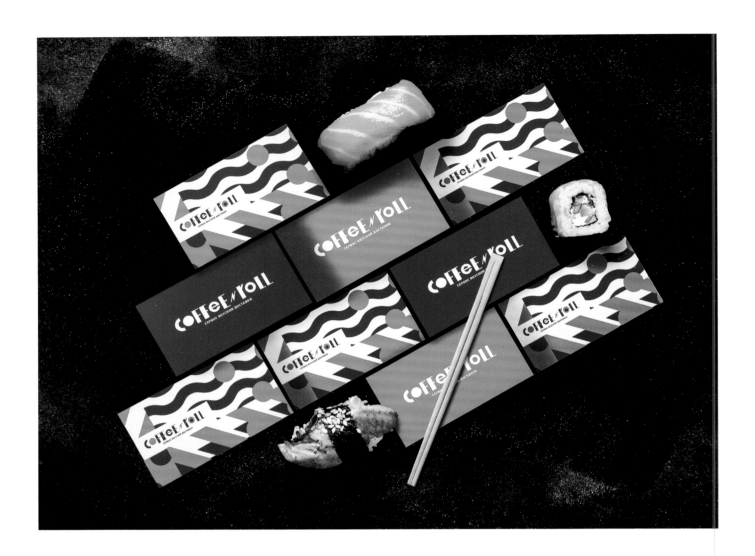

 C16 M73 Y54 K5 + C69 M22 Y0 K57

Japanese Food Delivery Service

Designer: Dmitry Neal
Client: Coffee&Roll

Coffee&Roll is a Japanese food delivery service. The company delivers coffee, sushi and rolls around the city in no time. Corporative style is based on a mix of colorful geometric shapes. Circles, diagonal stripes, waves present forms simplified to the maximum, with the reference to the main products and ingredients. To be exact, circles and diagonals represent fish whereas waves symbolize the sea. Graphics colour-code supports and emphasizes the main idea. The result is not a simple illustration to a Japanese theme, but a complex graphical reference on the level of feelings and associations.

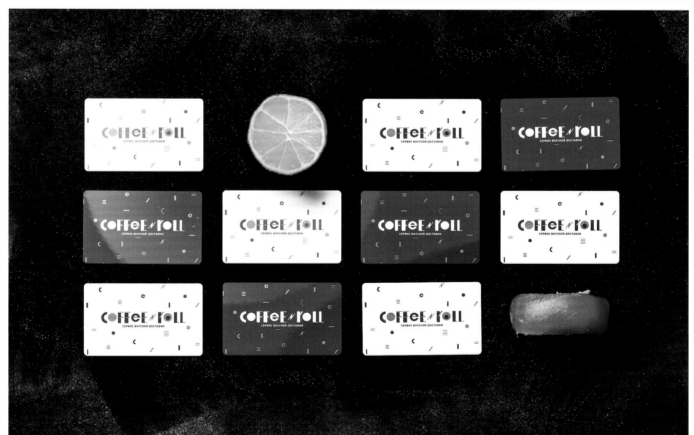

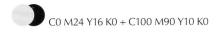 C0 M24 Y16 K0 + C100 M90 Y10 K0

New Port. In Centre

Designer: Justyna Radziej
Client: ŁAŹNIA Centre for Contemporary Art

New Port. In Centre (Nowy Port. W Centrum) is an educational programme created by Education Department from Laznia Centre for Contemporary Art to promote district of Gdańsk – Nowy Port, and to develop bond with its residents. The programme includes workshops, lectures and other cultural activities for children and adults. This design aimed to present in a clear and simple way an entire events agenda with description of each of them.

Podstawy filmu animowanego

luty – czerwiec 2017
Uczestnicy: **zorganizowane grupy szkolne**
Prowadzenie: **Robert Turło**
Zapisy: **warsztaty@laznia.pl**

Uczniowie pod okiem reżysera i scenarzysty filmowego zostaną wprowadzeni w podstawowe i klasyczne metody tworzenia filmów animowanych. Dzięki komputerom, podświetlanym pulpitom filmowym i specjalnemu oprogramowaniu będą mieli okazję do stworzenia własnej animacji.

Jeżeli jesteś nauczycielem zainteresowanym uczestnictwem Twojej klasy w bezpłatnych warsztatach, skontaktuj się z nami!

Animacja pikselacja
czyli animujemy obiektami trójwymiarowymi

25 – 26 marca 2017 | godz. 11.00 – 18.00
Uczestnicy: **młodzież, dorośli, seniorzy**
Prowadzenie: **Beata Bogucka i Robert Turło**
Zapisy: **kinoanimacja@laznia.pl**

Warsztaty tworzenia filmu animowanego metodą pikselacji zrealizowane zostaną w oparciu o poklatkowe zdjęcia wykonane wybranym obiektom i osobom. Animacja przedmiotem zostanie wzbogacona o przemyślane działanie światłem. W trakcie warsztatów zajmiemy się także trickową kompozycją obrazu oraz trickowym montażem.

Sztuka ziemi, ciała i umysłu

 PANTONE 197 UP + PANTONE 072 UP

Industry City Studios

Design Studio: Bardo Industries, LLC
Creative Director: Laura Giraudo
Designers: Laura Giraudo, Roberto Bernasconi
Client: Industry City

Industry City Studios is an artists and creators community located in Industry City, a complex of former warehouses on the Brooklyn waterfront.

On May 2017, over 100 artists, designers, and makers opened their doors including painters, photographers, sculptors, woodworkers, architects, jewelry and clothing designers, floral, textile and graphic designers. Also, there was artisanal food and beverage purveyors including specialty bakeries, whole-animal butchers, wine merchants, distilleries, and more.

Design Studio Bardo Industries were brought in to develop the Brand Identity for Industry City Studios, as well as the complete graphic universe for the event—an array of posters, postcards and more.

Industry City Studios

May 20th & 21st 2017 from 12pm to 6pm.

Over 100 artists, designers and makers will open their doors. Also opening will be artisan food and beverage purveyors including specialty bakeries, whole-animal butchers, wine merchants, distilleries, and more.

For more information, visit: www.industrycitystudios.org

Entrance: 254 36th Street, Brooklyn, NY 11232
Studio Buildings: 33rd Street to 39th Street between 2nd and 3rd Avenues
D, N, or R train to 36th Street
Bus: B71 to 3rd Avenue;
Car: BQE Exit 23 to 39th Street

Open Studios was made possible with the support of **Industry City.** www.industrycity.com

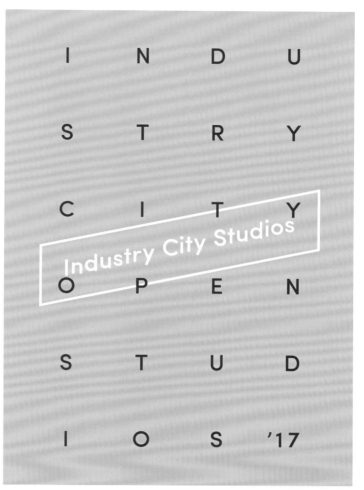

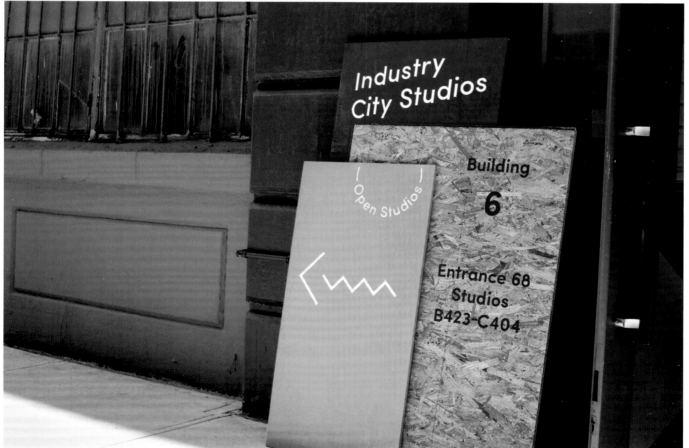

 PANTONE 805 + PANTONE Reflex Blue

FHP – University of Applied Sciences Potsdam

Design Studio: Formdusche
Creative Directors:
Svenja von Döhlen, Tim Finke, Timo Hummel, Steffen Wierer
Designer: Anja Bender
Client: University of Applied Sciences Potsdam

The newspaper-like information flyer for the Design and European Media Studies program at the University of Applied Sciences in Potsdam unconventionally clarifies all open questions about studies, course and career opportunities. And since you should not forget about playing, especially in the field of design, there is also room for a wink in one's eye. The back page is designed like a poster, fueling curiosity from afar and rewarding as readers approach with more details. The designers have chosen bright colour palette in order to grab the future students' attention.

C90 M20 Y0 K0 + C0 M15 Y0 K0

8×8 Con

Designer: YUKI INENAGA
Client: 1A PROJECT

8 x 8 Con is a bachelor party planned by the staff of a shipping company, which invites 8 men and 8 women to join and have fun. As the staff of shipping company use markers at work, the designer drew inspiration from this practice and made the typography resemble the handwriting of the markers. In Japan, there is a culture of colouring men and women by blue and red. Blue stands for men, and red stands for women. The overlapping of two colours suggests the encounter of participants.

Risograph Ink: Fluorescent Pink + Federal Blue

Our Golden Age of Pop Songs

Designer: Tun Ho
Client: Macao A Cappella Association

Macao A Cappella Association is formed by a group of people who love singing and A Cappella. Founded in 2011, they have presented songs of various genres as well as holding public performances, where they blended theatrical elements to make the show more interesting.

Designer Tun Ho was invited to design the tickets, brochure and posters for one of the performances, which, under the title of "Our Golden Age of Pop Songs", was to commemorate the popular songs that have affected Macao residents since the 1980s. The tickets and brochure were printed in Risograph to imitate the rustic texture of old-time theatre tickets, lending a nostalgic feeling, with which online tickets weren't comparable.

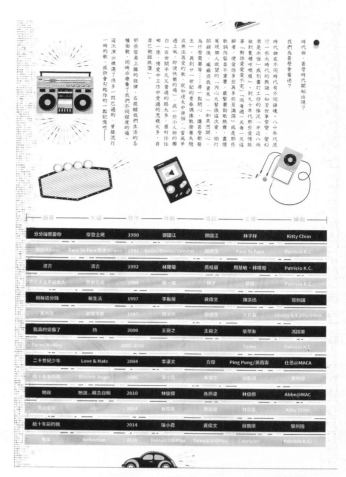

曲目	大碟	發行	作曲	填詞	主唱	編曲
分分鐘需要你	摩登土佬	1980	鄭國江	鄭國江	林子祥	Kitty Chim
情牽 Milano	Face To Face情牽Milano	1991	Davis/Bennu/Uozumi		Face To Face	Patricio K.C.
謊言	謊言	1992	林隆璇	黃桂蘭	周慧敏、林隆璇	Patricio K.C.
天生不容女人	吾家友會	1994	吳一偉	林夕	蘇樺	Patricio K.C.
抱擁這分鐘	新生活	1997	李焯雄	黃偉文	陳奕迅	葉創國
友共情	歡樂今會	1997	陳享明	崗楊院	古巨基	Jimmy & Kathy@MAC
我真的受傷了	熱	2000	王菲之	王菲之	張學友	馮國東
Twins Medley		2001-2005			Twins	Patricio K.C.
二十世紀少年	Love & Hate	2004	李漢文	方傑	Ping Pung/吳雨霏	仕思@MACA
幾十年後的我	Electric Angel	2006	陳小霞	蕭德堂	鍾凱琪	葉創國
她說	她說...概念自輯	2010	林俊傑	孫燕姿	林俊傑	Abbe@MAC
紅山後祥	<3	2014	林憶蓮	陳詠謙	林二汶	Kitty Chim
給十年前的我		2014	陳小霞	黃偉文	薛凱琪	葉創國
倒影	Reflection	2016	Tomy@100Plus	Tomy@100Plus	Catalyser	Patricio K.C.

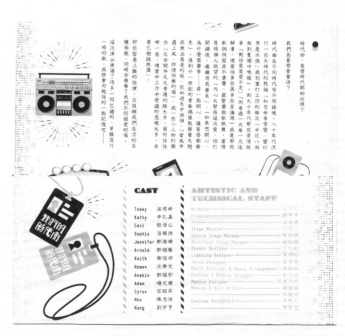

CAST

Tobey 溫倩婷
Kathy 卓孔嘉
Ceci 戴倩仙
Sophia 湯穎詩
Jennifer 鄭端璋
Arnold 鄧越隆
Keith 謝信祥
Homen 沈學文
Anakin 鄧越彤
Adam 楊文暉
Cyrus 容駿昇
Hou 陳志浩
Hang 劉宇亨

ARTISTIC AND TECHNICAL STAFF

Director .... 古英元
Producer .... 劉宇亨
Stage Manager .... 溫倩婷
Deputy Stage Manager .... 卓孔嘉
Assistant Stage Manager .... 陳欣穎
Scenic Designer .... 丁俊傑
Lighting Designer .... 陳棨楊
Sound Designer .... 謝信祥
Music Director & Music Arrangement .... 陳嘉誠
Costume & Makeup Designer .... 李子洛
Makeup Designer .... 梁倩瑜
Makeup & Hair Artist .... 李倩瑜
Costume Assistant .... 黃雪雯

 C85 M71 Y0 K0 + C0 M62 Y41 K0

Book Marathon

Design Studio: azul recreo
Creative and Art Directors: Mateo Buitrago, Elisa Piquer
Photographer: Seiyu
Client: Book Marathon

Book Marathon is a project which turns any book into a literary race track where only the quickest eyes can win. To start, each reader must choose the bookmark he likes the most, a book through which to run and read until his character wins the race. Every bookmark includes its own medal table to keep the badges obtained with each victory. Notebooks have lists in which readers can record their races results, new words they've learned or favorite quotes. This project seeks to promote reading habits in children, presenting books as what they are – something fun.

The designers chose blue and red as the main colours because they were looking for a nostalgic touch. These colours reminded them of wooden toys from childhood, primary colours but worn out because of the time. The blue and red also build a linguistic code that differentiates the two product languages: English (blue) and Spanish (red).

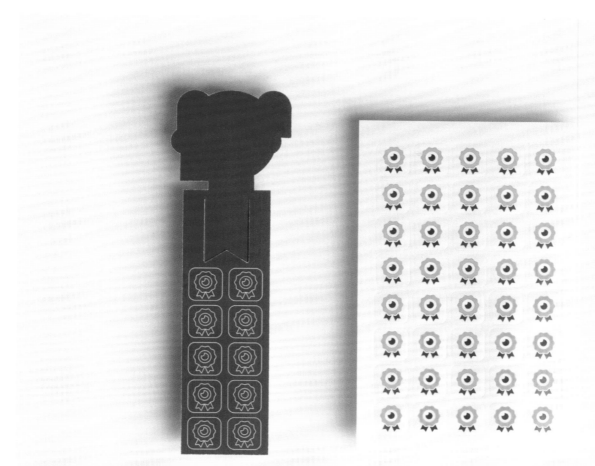

Pol

He is the youngest of the four. He is always running around.

In the evenings after school he does what he likes most: devouring books and eating. He is curious and is a joker and adventurer.

Jess

Once she realised that roller-skating was just like sliding around the floor of her house in her socks, she decided she'd never take her skates off again.

She goes right through any book she comes across. She is fun and unrelenting. She accepts any challenge.

PANTONE 7417 U + PANTONE 5517 U

Season's Greetings

Design Studio: Thinking Room
Designer: Evan Wijaya

Every year Thinking Room, a Jakarta-based graphic design studio, would give its clients a sort of Christmas hampers along with a Christmas card attached. In 2017, the Christmas card design tried to evoke a classic feel of traditional Christmas cards but with a twist. The studio came up with an idea to make Santa's Nice List and attached the list inside every single card. The cards were personalized by putting the clients' names into the Nice List along with the names of some famous graphic designers. The list functioned as a kind of replica of the "real" Santa's Nice List, made by Santa Claus and approved by Mrs. Claus herself. Some nice colours were picked from vintage Christmas cards to invoke the classic vibe of traditional Christmas cards. Green and red were chosen but was made less vibrant.

C2 M86 Y100 K0 + C50 M80 Y80 K6

Mama Mafia

Design Studio: Openmint / *Creative Director:* Dmitry Zhelnov
Designer: Katerina Teterkina / *Visualisation:* Yegor Kumachov
Client: Mama Mafia

Mama Mafia is a delivery service which specializes in Italian and
Japanese cuisines. The concept of the service is a mix of the home-taste
food, the delivery speed which is faster than a bullet from the Tommy
gun, and a strict quality control that could even win the heart of Yakuza.

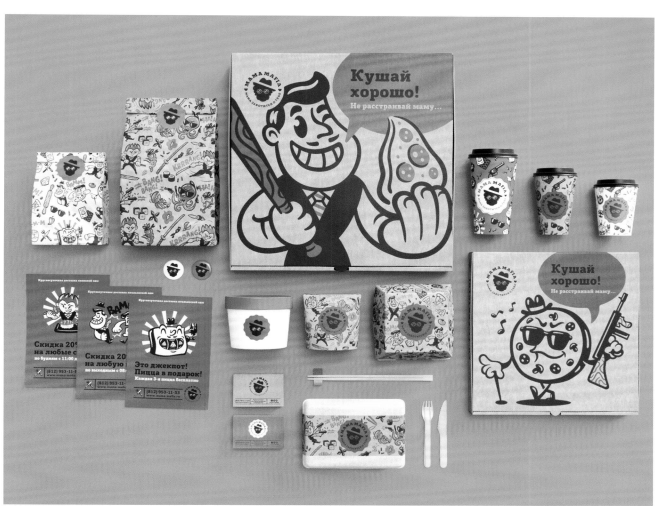

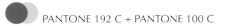

PANTONE 192 C + PANTONE 100 C

Sun Festival

Designer: Attila Hadnagy
Credit: The Sun Festival Team (www.sun-festival.org)

One of the projects of the MarocK'Jeunes association, the Sun Festival is Marrakech's International Music Festival. It involves establishment of different international organizations for the promotion of universal ideals of peace, freedom and equality. During the last nine editions, a variety of artists from different countries met up in Marrakech via a rich program of events, contemporary art, conferences, training programs, exhibitions and many concerts.

Attila Hadnagy was commissioned to re-design the Sun Festival's logo and branding. This is one of the design concept he did for the festival. The logo idea came from Marrakech's beautiful sunset. The goal was to create a vibrant and energetic look for the festival, which is why he chose and combined the red and yellow colour combination.

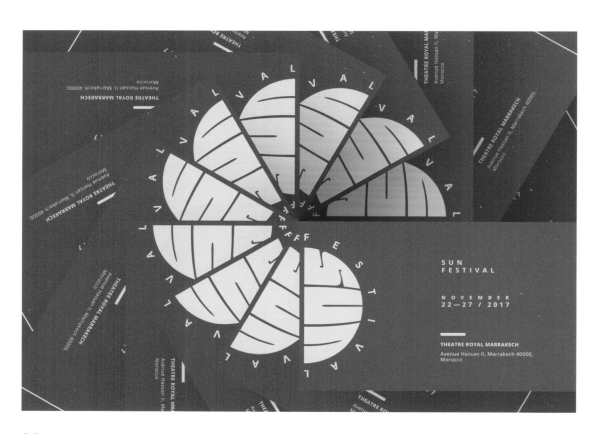

FESTIVAL

FESTIVAL
BOOK
2017

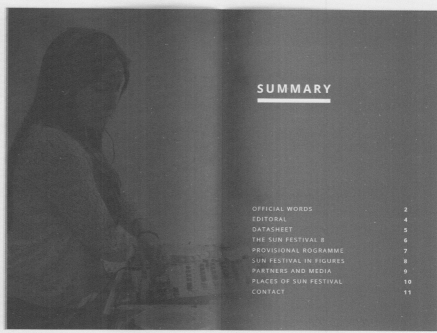

SUMMARY

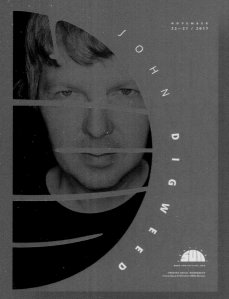

R122 G240 B218 + R255 G24 B5

Tropical Lighthouse

Designer: Robert Bazaev
Client: LAST 9

LAST 9 is a music blog without any genre limitations. Its distinctive feature is drop-shape covers and connection between music and visual component. LAST 9 produces conceptual compilations, each containing main theme reflected in music mood and visual concept.

Tropical Lighthouse is the 15th compilation of a series. Cover, promo video and vinyl disc packing were designed within this project. The project was inspired by tunes and sounds of tropical forest, and the main musical inspiration is oeuvre of the musician and artist Mtendere Mandowa, famous under his stage name Teebs. His music contains special beats and vibrations combined with light vibe of retro, creating alien landscapes in imagination. The design concept is based on recognizable symbol of a drop, serving as a source of light and a lighthouse that emit light on the area around itself. Important feature of Tropical Lighthouse is a combination of two bright tones. Bright turquoise and scarlet colours are in harmony creating deep contrast with each other.

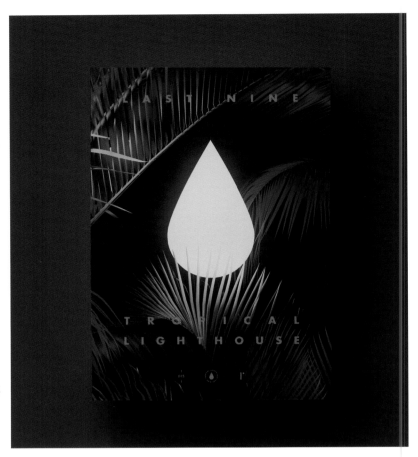

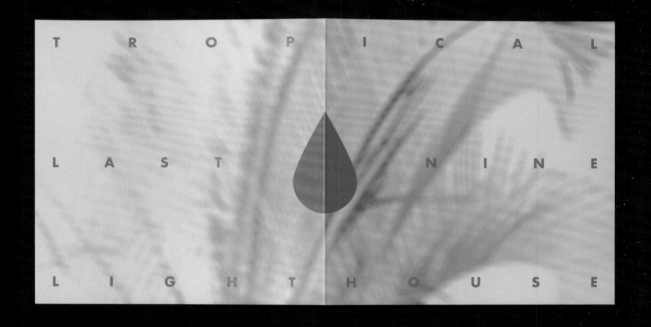

T R O P I C A L

L A S T   N I N E

L I G H T H O U S E

A

DAEDELUS – VOUS EYES STEREO

PERERA ELSEWHERE – DRUNK MAN
(PREFUSE 73 AA MEDITATION MIX)

TEEBS – TOP HATS

MACHINEDRUM – BELLSEA

B

PERERA ELSEWHERE & BASS SEKOLAH – POLARIS

TAKE – YOU HIGH (DAEDELUS REMIX)

HOMINIDAE – EACH & ALL

SONS OF THE MORNING – THE WAY THAT WINTER PASSED US

TEEBS – VIEW POINT

 C100 M0 Y100 K0 + C0 M100 Y100 K0

Ternana Marathon Club

Design Studio: Bocanegra Studio
Creative Directors: Roberto Sensi, Sara Marigliani
Designers: Roberto Sensi, Sara Marigliani
Client: Tommaso Moroni, Ternana Marathon Club

The project contains logo and visual identity designed for Ternana Marathon Club, running team based in Terni, Italy. For the logo, Bocanegra Studio took inspiration from the Olympic torch, the marathon iconic symbol, where the torch is represented by the letter T (for Ternana) with a stylized flame on top.
The logo comes in two versions. The first one is like an emblem, with a full colour background used primarily on clothing and accessories. The second one is more synthetic, composed by the torch-like symbol with the typography on the side.

The colour palette is composed of red and green, colours of the city of Terni and of the Ternana F.C. The Studio aimed to create a visual identity based on a strong symbol representing the core value of the athletes of Ternana Marathon Club, using a simple and modern language and a significant set of primary colours.

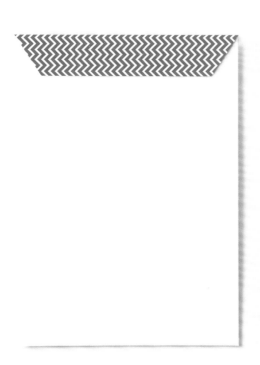

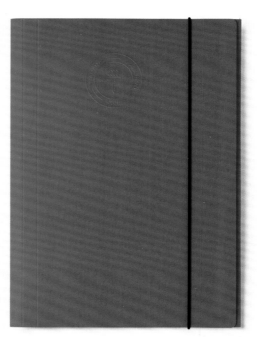

 PANTONE 3288 + PANTONE 805

Barcelona Jewish Film Festival

Design Studio: Familia
Creative Director: Aleix Artigal
Designer: Aleix Artigal
Client: Barcelona Jewish Film Festival

The annual Barcelona Jewish Film Festival hosts Jewish films and films related to Jewish culture. The initials C and J (Jewish Film, or "Cinema Jueu" in Catalan), with its abstract and geometric shapes, were inspired by the Hebrew alphabet and comprised the frame of the festival's films. These two typographic forms became flexible elements that unify all the communication pieces within the graphic space. The proportions of the letters were adapted to the dimensions of each usage, which allows for applications in different formats without losing the graphic identity.

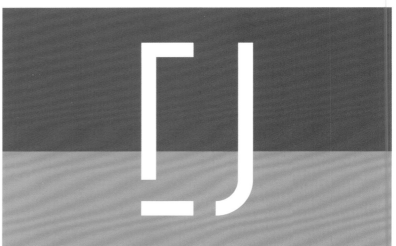

C60 M100 Y0 K0 + C0 M60 Y100 K0

Week van de Amateurkunsten

Designers: Kevin Brenkman, Bibi Kelder, Tijn Bakker
Projects conducted at LUCA School of the Arts, Belgium

Week van de Amateurkunsten (Week of the Amateur Arts) is a yearly event held throughout Belgium. The theme of 2018 was Kunst Buiten (Art Outside) and was all about coming out with your work.

The designers wanted to represent the theme in the posters and social media campaign, so they created multiple posters in two separate layers. The bottom layer is the actual poster displaying the information, while the top layer is changing in all posters. A poster that is partly visible or obscured would trigger the curiosity of the viewer to wonder what exactly the poster is for. In other mediums they looked for different solutions to visualize this idea. In social media posts, the top layer gets brushed away. In print work, certain information was hidden by a scratching layer. The viewer has to make the information appear by scratching away the foil.

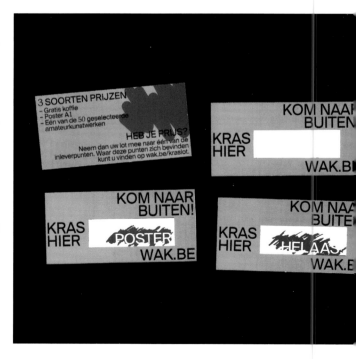

KOM NAAR BUITEN!
27.04-06.05.18
WEEK VAN DE AMATEUR KUNSTEN

WAK.BE

KOM NAAR BUITEN
27.04.18–06.05.18
WEEK VAN DE AMATEURKUNSTEN

De Week van de Amateurkunsten is dé jaarlijkse kunstweek in Vlaanderen en Brussel. Van vrijdag 27 april t.e.m. zondag 6 mei 2018 tonen we de kracht van zelf kunst maken. Met twee miljoen zijn ze, de acteurs, fotografen, dichters, schilders, muzikanten, tekenaars, performers, schrijvers, zangers, filmmakers en dansers die uit passie en goesting kunst beoefenen in hun vrije tijd. Tijdens de Week van de Amateurkunsten tonen ze hun werk aan het brede publiek.

Met het jaarthema leggen we telkens een focus. KUNST BUITEN! gaat over kunst in de publieke ruimte, naar buiten komen met je kunst, je kunst binnenste buiten halen, maar ook over de plaats van kunst binnen het (lokale) cultuurbeleid en binnen onze samenleving. En je kunt altijd buiten de lijntjes kleuren...

EVENTS

1 DIGITAL STREET ART (R)ESTART REALITY BRUSSEL
Breng buitenkunst tot leven met je smartphone. Zoek in Petite Rue des Bouchers/Kleine Beenhouwersstraat, Place d'Espagne/Spanjeplein, Rue du Marché aux Peaux/Huidenmarkt en Bozar voor karakters van 100 jaar geleden.

2 15E BIENNALE DEINSE KUNSTENAARS DEINZE
Deze groepstentoonstelling biedt de bezoeker een totaaloverzicht op wat er in Deinze leeft op het artistieke vlak. Aan de vorige edities namen telkens meer dan 75 kunstenaars deel, die ongeveer 150 werken exposeerden, waaronder enkele bijzondere blikvangers. Iedereen uit Deinze (wonen, werken of studeren) die artistiek werk wil tonen, kan zich kandidaat stellen tot eind dit jaar. 15e Biennale...

3 FEEST VAN DE FOLK GOOIK
Muziekmozaïek viert al haar zestiende editie van het Feest van de Folk toe en dit volledig binnen de Week van de Amateurkunsten. Gedurende 10 dagen worden dan in heel Vlaanderen en Brussel tientallen folkactiviteiten opgezet door diverse organisatoren.

4 KUNST BUITEN, CONCERT LONDERZEEL
9 groepen samenspel treden samen op. Alle groepen spelen 1 werk en samen spelen ze een groot gezamenlijk slotstuk.

5 WORKSHOP ACRYL KERMT
Tijdens deze korte workshop krijg je heel concrete demonstraties en kleurmogelijkheden om een mooi abstract landschap te creëren. Je krijgt de mogelijkheid om je kleuren te testen, techniek te oefenen en gebruik te maken van combinaties zoals collages.

6 REPETITIE POPKOOR IOCA OP ZONDAG OELEGEM
Het popkoor ioca, wat ioca betekent, is een projectkoor met ambitie, met telkens een nieuw en modern repertoire. Het koor bestaat uit gemotiveerde koorleden. Hun ervaring, creativiteit, gevoel voor humor en enthousiasme brengt ioca waar het wil zijn: in de zevende hemel. Ioca is uniek. Het plezier van het zingen komt op de allereerste plaats. Want wie zich goed voelt, zingt beter.

7 CULTUURHAPPENING 2018 OVERPELT
De Overpeltse Cultuurraad organiseert een nieuwe editie van de Cultuurhappening. In het kader hiervan geeft de Cultuurraad in de tentoonstellingsruimten van CC Palethe kans aan lokaal talent om hun werk te tonen. Ook werken van amateurkunstenaars worden in deze tentoonstelling betrokken.

8 KUNSTROUTE, OPEN ATELIERS
Verschillende kunstenaars uit de gemeente Ravels zullen deelnemen aan een kunstroute waarbij velen hun atelier openstellen. Allerhande kunstvormen komen op deze twee-daagse aan bod.

9 CABERDOUCHE TONEELVERENIGING DE VLAAMSE HARTEN
Iedereen die al eens ooit na een avondje stappen met een groep vrienden in de omgeving van die leuke buurt is beland, weet dat er wel wat te beleven valt in de plaatselijke cafeetjes. Ambiance verzekerd en 't kantje. Hoertjes, pooiers, travesties, zestol en andere meestal.

10 SLOTCONCERT WEEK VAN DE AMATEURKUNSTEN TESSENDERLO
Jaarlijks concert van de Koninklijke harmonie St-Lucia uit Engsbergen in OC 't Goor te Engsbergen.

11 KUNST IN DE ETALAGE, INGRID FEVERY MALDEGEM
Tijdens de Week van de Amateurkunsten worden kunstwerken tentoongesteld in de centrumvitrines van Ingrid Fevery.

VIND ALLE EVENTS OP WAK.BE

27.04	28.04	29.04	30.04	01.05	02.05	03.05	04.05	05.05	06.05.18

 PANTONE 874 C + PANTONE 2089 C

Arttravellers Exhibition Series I: Decoding Exotic Land

Design Studio: Good Morning Design
Creative Director: Jim Wong
Designer: Jim Wong
Client: Art Promotion Office (APO)

Visual Identity for the exhibition # Arttravellers Exhibition Series I: Decoding Exotic Lands, organised by Art Promotion Office(APO). The exhibitions invite a number of local artists to look into the culture of modern travel among Hong Kong people and discover its possibility and variety, offering the audience an alternative perspective on the inattentive culture and anecdotes that visitors have often missed in the journey. Featuring two local young female artists, the exhibition looks into the exotic signs connecting with the different experience and impressions of travel of them. Violet and copper colour were used to symbolize the atmosphere of the exoticism. The kaleidoscope-like graphics illustrated as windows for audiences to explore the exotic icons discovered by the artists.

#藝術旅人展覽系列一
#ArtTravellers Exhibition Series I

異國符號

DECODING EXOTIC LANDS

鄭淑宜 Eastman Cheng × Ivy Ma 馬琼珠

24|2 → 23|8|2017

香港九龍協調道3號工業貿易大樓一樓大堂
1/F Lobby, Trade and Industry Tower,
3 Concorde Road, Kowloon, Hong Kong

開放時間 Opening hours
星期一至五 Mon to Fri： 9:00am – 6:00pm
星期六 Sat： 9:00am – 2:00pm
逢星期日及公眾假期休息
Closed on Sundays and Public Holidays

f ⓞ apo.arttravellers

主辦 Presented by
康樂及文化事務署
Leisure and Cultural Services Department

策劃 Organised by
«a po
藝術推廣辦事處
ART PROMOTION OFFICE

 PANTONE 2935 U + PANTONE 873 U

TIFF 2017 Annual Report

Design Studio: Blok Design
Creative Directors: Vanessa Eckstein, Marta Cutler
Designers: Vanessa Eckstein, Jaclyn Hudson
Client: Toronto International Film Festival (TIFF)

The 2017 annual report is a love letter to cinema and an ode to one of the world's most renowned and respected cinematic organizations. To capture the core of what makes Toronto International Film Festival (TIFF) so unique, the designers paired bold verbs with unexpected concepts, such as "Catalyze collectivity", "Inspire time" and "Shift dreams/reality". This poetic tribute inspired the rest of the design, which eschews conventional format and embraces the beauty and language of film to create a cinematic experience that amplifies TIFF's mission to transform how people see the world through film.

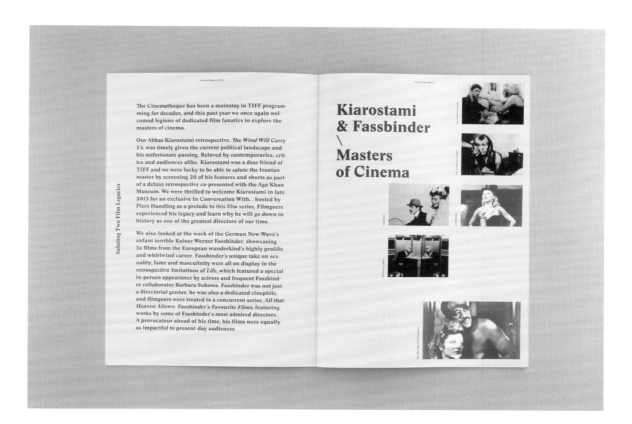

The Cinematheque has been a mainstay in TIFF programming for decades, and this past year we once again welcomed legions of dedicated film fanatics to explore the masters of cinema.

Our Abbas Kiarostami retrospective, *The Wind Will Carry Us*, was timely given the current political landscape and his unfortunate passing. Beloved by contemporaries, critics and audiences alike, Kiarostami was a dear friend of TIFF and we were lucky to be able to salute the Iranian master by screening 20 of his features and shorts as part of a deluxe retrospective co-presented with the Aga Khan Museum. We were thrilled to welcome Kiarostami in late 2015 for an exclusive In Conversation With... hosted by Piers Handling as a prelude to this film series. Filmgoers experienced his legacy and learn why he will go down in history as one of the greatest directors of our time.

We also looked at the work of the German New Wave's enfant terrible Rainer Werner Fassbinder, showcasing 36 films from the European wunderkind's highly prolific and whirlwind career. Fassbinder's unique take on sexuality, fame and masculinity were all on display in the retrospective *Imitations of Life*, which featured a special in-person appearance by actress and frequent Fassbinder collaborator Barbara Sukowa. Fassbinder was not just a directorial genius; he was also a dedicated cinephile, and filmgoers were treated to a concurrent series, *All that Heaven Allows: Fassbinder's Favourite Films*, featuring works by some of Fassbinder's most admired directors. A provocateur ahead of his time, his films were equally as impactful to present-day audiences.

Saluting Two Film Legacies

Kiarostami & Fassbinder
\ Masters of Cinema

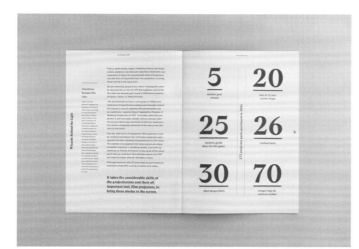

 Risograph Ink: Fluorescent Orange + Gold

2018 Chinese
New Year Card

Designer: Chen, Hao-En

Good things happen in the new year. White rice symbolizes wealth, and the meaning of sending rice is giving good wishes to each other, hoping them could have sustained financial resources and no worries of food and clothing. With a heartfelt blessing, the designer passes on good wishes to everyone who is full of warmth and full of happiness.

Orange stands for warm beauty, the festival of happiness and joy. Gold represents extravagance, a symbol of wheat, sunshine, plentiful money and treasure.

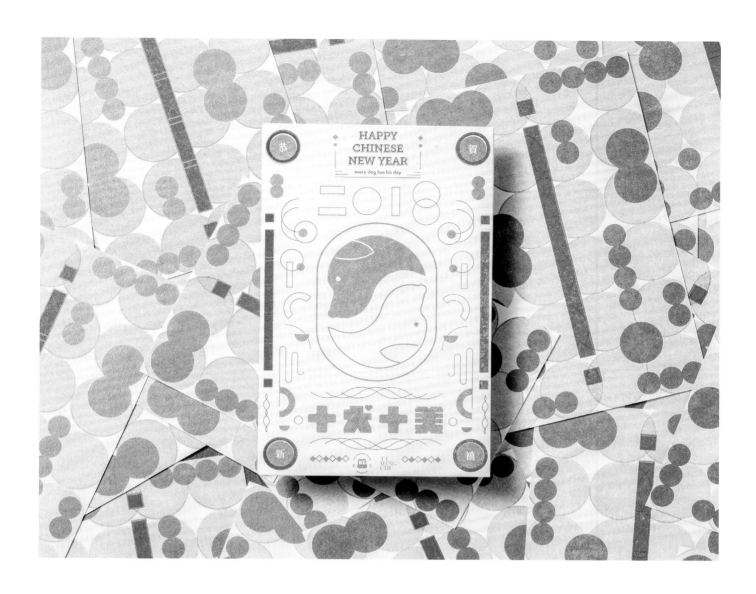

 Risograph Ink: Green 40% & 100% +
Metallic Gold 40% & 100%

2O18 Chinese New Year of Dog |
Branch Beats The Dog

Design Studio: Ti-Ming Chu Workshop
Designer: Ti-Ming Chu
Risograph Printing: O.OO Risograph & Design Room

As a fan of Stephen Chow, the designer Ti-Ming Chu takes inspiration from Chow's movie "King of Beggars" and the most important item from the Beggars' Sect, "Branch Beats the Dog", which originated from martial arts writer Jin Yong. When beggars beg on the streets, they encounter well-off people who disrespect them. And this is why they carry a branch, to protect themselves from those who think they are better than anyone else.

In 2018, the year of the dog, the designer presented this project to his audience with the sincere hope: stay true to yourself and live a stress-free life. If they are thinking about getting a dog, consider adopting rather than purchasing.

HIP HOP CITOYENS PRÉSENTE

PARIS HIP HOP WINTER

Du **02** au **11**
DÉCEMBRE
2016

CONCERT · CINÉMA · CONFÉRENCE

Avant-première du film
LES DERNIERS PARISIENS
réalisé et produit par
LA RUMEUR

BIZARRE RIDE LIVE !
Feat. SLIMKID3, L.A JAY,
J-SWIFT & K-NATURAL
Formerly of **THE PHARCYDE**

ESPIIEM
présente ORFÈVRE LABEL

**JOSMAN / O'BOY
TAKE A MIC / MAKALA**

CHEEKO & BLANKA
Feat. YOSHI & SOAP / PEPSO STAVINSKY
DEGIHEUGI (LIVE BEATMAKING)

FINALE **BUZZ BOOSTER** IDF#7

CREA : KEBBA SANNEH · MATHIEU DELESTRE

 C0 M85 Y52 K0 + C95 M95 Y30 K0

Paris Hip Hop
Winter Festival 2016

Creative Directors: BuröNeko, Kebba Sanneh
Designer: Mathieu Delestre
Illustrator: Kebba Sanneh
Client: Paris Hip Hop

Paris Hip Hop Winter Festival serves as an extension of the main Paris Hip Hop Festival held in summer. The idea is to lay the foundation of a new kind of meeting dedicated to Hip Hop, which is based on music, cinema, and all the concerns of Hip Hop culture, practices and arts.

For the poster, the designers were looking for an animal representing winter, which should have a strong character but less aggressive stance. That's how they chose bear as the main character. In terms of colour palette, instead of applying the common colours of cyan, white and light blue to fit the theme of winter, they made use of red and blue to achieve the eye-catching outcome.

 C0 M20 Y94 K0 + C100 M89 Y19 K4

Paris Hip Hop 2017

Creative Directors: BuröNeko, Kebba Sanneh
Designer: Mathieu Delestre
Illustrator: Kebba Sanneh
Client: Paris Hip Hop

Paris Hip Hop 2017 is the 12th edition of the main Paris Hip Hop Festival, which is a project featuring both local and international Hip Hop artists.

Followed along the poster designed for the Paris Hip Hop winter festival, which shown on the left page, the designers stayed on the animal theme to represent the energy of Hip Hop Movement. They traduced its virulence and anti-establishment spirit by a bestial clash. Two clear-cut colours, yellow and blue, were applied to create a warm atmosphere.

PANTONE 803 C +
PANTONE Reflex Blue C

Chamboule Tout!

Mentor: Atelier AAAAA
Designers: Onss Mhirsi, Marine Dion, Anaelle Barnier, Marie Anne Barjoux
School Project at École supérieure Estienne des Arts et Industries graphiques, Paris, France

Chamboule tout! is an art direction proposal for The Trophée Presse Citron BnF. French press drawing contest co-organized by l'École Estienne and the BnF (Bibliotheque Nationale de France). The main concept was to be as punchy as a press drawing. The designing team wanted this proposal to articulate a violent and powerful message throughout the use of bold typography and over-saturated colours with high impact.

 PANTONE 109 C + PANTONE 2756 C

Giro Festival

Designer: Dacil Sánchez

Giro festival intends to give traditional festivals a "twist" ("Giro", in Spanish) by alternating yoga workshops during the day with indie music concerts at night, which make it different and unique. The identity explores the idea of creating opposing environments that will change according to the sunlight and moonlight. It is similarly based on other dual concepts such as yin and yang, speed and slowness, sound and silence or a "U" turn. To reflect this principal idea of antagonistic concepts visually, nothing is better than the use of complementary colours. In this case, yellow and purple blue have been used, giving the duotone importance and thus creating a great contrast. Yellow is used in representation of the yoga related activities taking place during daytime, as it evokes light and sun. In contrast, purple blue defines the night and is used for the branding of the music concerts.

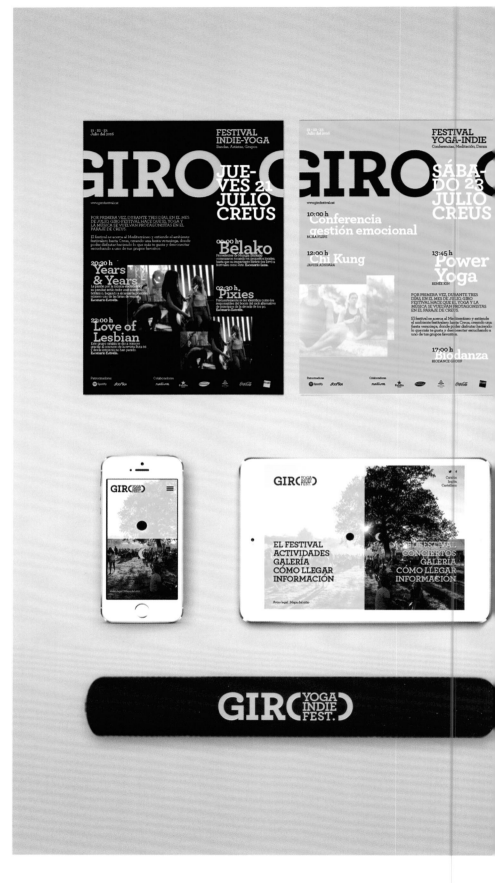

GIR◯◯◯ 21-23 julio ⟩⟩⟩⟩⟩

GIR◯◯◯ sábado 21 ⟩⟩⟩⟩⟩

GIR◯◯◯ 21-23 julio ⟩⟩⟩⟩⟩

GIR◯◯◯ 00006

I

Instructora
Aguirina Vegas
Experta en Sahaja Yoga

G
O

GIRO
GIRO

21 - 23
JULIO
CREUS

---

21 - 22 - 23
Julio del 2016

FESTIVAL YOGA-INDIE
Festival Giro actividades de yoga
y música indie.

GIRO

21-23 JULIO CREUS

www.girofestival.cat

JUE-VES 21

10:00 h
Conferencia Thai
Yoga Massage
Este masaje tailandés tradicional tiene
sus orígenes en la India hace unos 2.500
años, en los tiempos de la medicina
ayurvédica y el yoga.

12:00 h
AcroYoga
Relájate fusionando el yoga, la acrobacia
y las artes terapéuticas. Es la mezcla de
estos tres linajes lo que permite hacer
posible lo imposible.

15:00 h
Amrita Yoga
Las enseñanzas espirituales como la
necesidad de desarrollar la conciencia,
los valores universales como la no
violencia, la verdad y la devoción,
forman parte de sus cimientos.

17:00 h
Dragon Dance
Yin Yang Yoga
La danza del dragón es un flujo
elegante y de gran alcance que nos hará
cuestionar todo nuestro ser.

20:30 h
Years & Years
La pasión por la música electrónica
y su peculiar estilo indie unió a este
trío británico, llegando a alcanzar la
posición número uno de las listas de
ventas.

22:00 h
Love of Lesbian
Este grupo catalán se dio a conocer
gracias al concurso de la revista Ruta 66
y desde entonces no han parado.

00:00 h
Belako
Procedentes de Mungia (Bizkaia)
comenzaron tocando en pequeños
locales, hasta que su impactante directo
les llevó a festivales como éste.

02:30 h
Pixies
Frecuentemente se les identifica como
los responsables del boom del rock
alternativo de principios de la década
de los 90.

VIER-NES 22

10:00 h
Yoga Ocular
El sentido de la vista es el que nos
proporciona mayor información del
entorno y, quizás, el más activo en el
lenguaje corporal.

11:30 h
Yoga en parejas
El Yoga en pareja es una forma de
aprender a confiar en esa persona. Si un
yogui está sobre otro mientras hacen
una postura y el de abajo falla, cae.

14:00 h
Meditación
El objetivo principal de la meditación
es concentrarse y relajar la mente hasta
liberar la conciencia.

17:00 h
Sahaja Yoga
Hoy Sahaja Yoga se practica en los
5 continentes, en todos los países
democráticos que admiten libertad de
culto y de creencias.

01:00 h
John Berkhout
Sus cinco miembros pasaron del sonido
hippie folk psicodélico a protagonizar
otros más acústicos.

Inheaven
Se trata de un cuarteto musical que
mezcla himnos indie atmosféricos,
guitarras y pegadizas composiciones.

21:00 h
Russian Red
Es una cantautora de indie, folk y pop
que, con su dulce voz y sus letras, ha
conseguido emocionar a su público.

23:00 h
Izal
Un trío de amigos que empezaron a
tocar con tan solo 13 años y que hoy
realiza innumerables giras, actuando en
diferentes escenarios, auditorios, etc.

SABA-DO 23

10:00 h
Conferencia
gestión emocional
Aprende a regular las propias
emociones. Gestionarlas, canalizarlas y
positivarlas forma parte de la esencia de
la vida de las personas.

12:00 h
Chi Kung
Es una terapia medicinal de origen
chino basada en el control de la
respiración. Ayuda a eliminar las
tensiones y el estrés.

13:45 h
Power Yoga
Las posturas de Power Yoga están
basadas en secuencias que los
profesores adaptan a cada nuevo
practicante, haciéndolas más avanzadas
o más sencillas.

17:00 h
Biodanza
Es un sistema de "auto-desarrollo",
que utiliza los sentimientos provocados
por la música y el movimiento para
profundizar en la conciencia de uno
mismo.

19:45 h
Kasabian
Es un grupo inglés cuyo estilo musical
es el rock, aunque en sus álbumes han
reflejado otros estilos, como el indie.

22:00 h
Arctic Monkeys
Son cuatro chicos ingleses de Sheffield
que resultaron una revelación en 2005,
al contrario que muchas otras bandas de
rock, aún no han caído en el olvido.

00:30 h
The Killers
En 2001 se formó esta banda musical.
En un principio apostó por el rock pero,
en los últimos años, ha cambiado su
estilo hacia el electro pop y post punk
alternativo.

02:30 h
Delorean
Es una banda vasca formada en el año
2000. Se ha convertido, por méritos
propios, en uno de los grupos más
interesantes de la escena nacional.

Patrocinadores
Spotify · YOGI TEA

Colaboradores
natura · Estrella Damm · Provamel · MAYAN YOGA · Coca-Cola · fnac

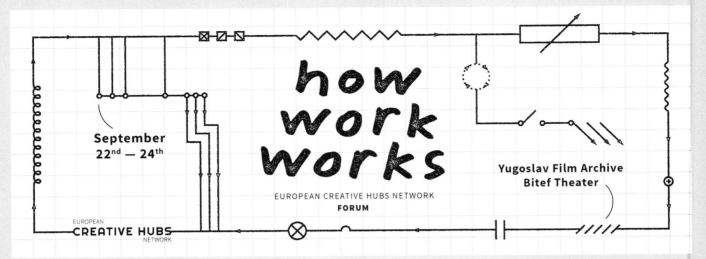

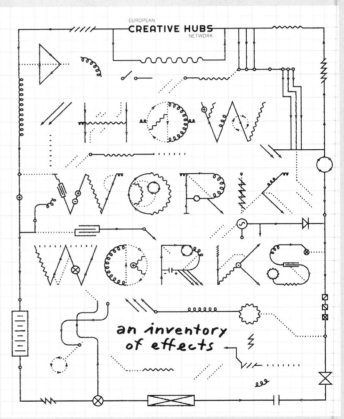

PANTONE 1205 U + PANTONE 280 U

How Work Works Conference

Design Studio: Nova Iskra Studio
Creative Director: Olga Jorgacevic
Designers: Olga Jorgacevic, Andreja Miric
Photographer: Nemanja Knezevic
Client: Culture Code

The international forum "How Work Works" was part of the European Creative Hubs Network project initiated by the British Council, co-funded by the European Commission through the Creative Europe program. Nova Iskra Studio contributed to the conference with a number of creative solutions—from visual identity, space branding, printed material, through PR, communication and marketing, to the event production. The visual identity reflected the theme of the forum—the future of work, which is also why a blue and yellow colour palette was used, and graphics were drawn inspiration from vintage blueprints. Instead of making an array of flyers and catalogs, they opted for a book format catalog, which also featured critical texts related to the topic and a selection of artworks that resonate with the topic by their collaborator Dušan Rajić, and featured a detachable program flyer.

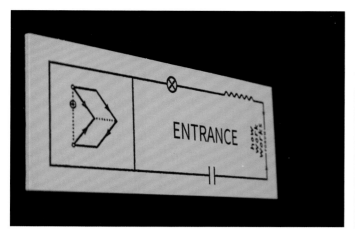

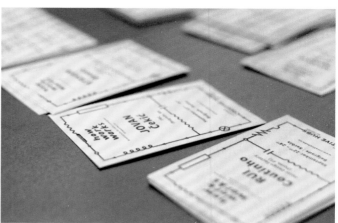

 PANTONE 7550 + PANTONE Blue 072

UdeM's 2017 Back-to-School Campaign

Design Studio: Gauthier
Creative Directors: Shawn Bedford, Nathalie Vézina
Designers: Alix Neyvoz, Clément Fusil
Photographer: Christian Blais
Illustrator: Sébastien Thibault
Client: Université de Montréal

Every new semester at Université de Montréal bustles with thousands of young adults reconnecting with student life. In the new semester of 2017, seven iconic ambassadors welcomed the crowd: the creative, the new, the festive, the sport-minded, the committed, the economical and the explorer. Thanks to stunning visuals, students readily identified with their alter ego and many engaged proudly in their new-found community.

Tempo Doeloe Typeface

Designer: Evan Wijaya

Tempo Doeloe, meaning "Old Times", is a mix between the Western Art Deco and the traditional Indonesian Javanese Script. The inspiration of the typeface came from letters that were used on old signages on buildings and public places in Indonesia in the past, especially during the Dutch colonialism era. Around 1920-1930s, the West was on the zeitgeist of the Art Deco era. It was so popular at that time that the Dutch also brought the Art Deco influence to Indonesia. This can be seen through the vintage Indonesian postcards, advertisements, signages, and architecture. Some of the design mixed the traditional culture of Indonesia with the Art Deco style and the results were amazing.

Inspired by the same process, Tempo Doeloe was made as a synthesis of the aforementioned Western type and the Javanese Script, made to complete the modern need of retro display text. In conjunction with the typeface design, many other implementations of the typeface were made, such as posters, postcards, pattern design, packaging labels, and more. The use of the two prominent colours in the design was meant to invoke the vintage nuances of Indonesia's past times.

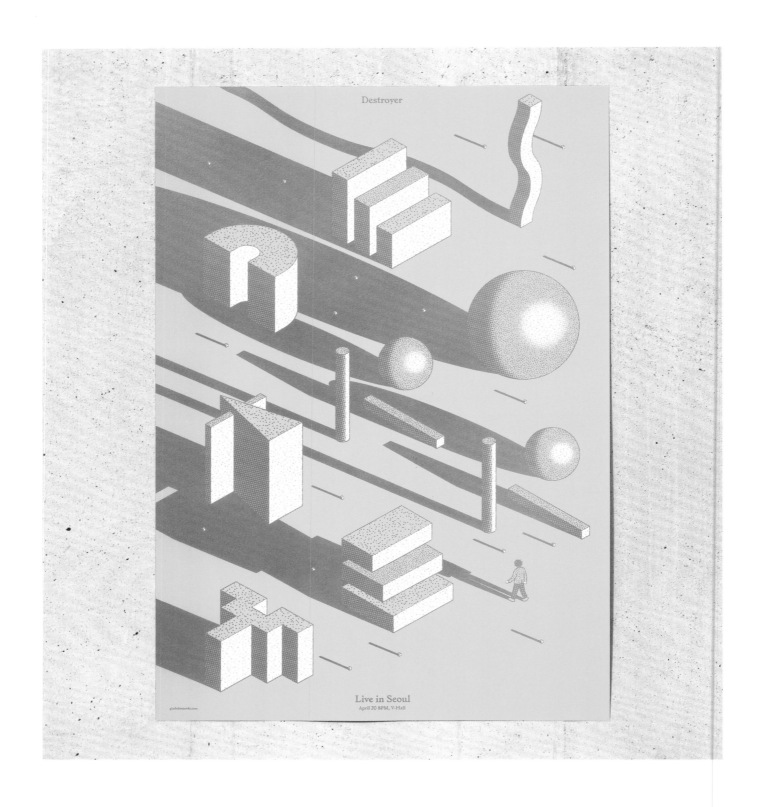

 PANTONE 803 + Gold

Destroyer: 2016 Live in Seoul

Designer: Jaemin Lee
Client: Gimbab Records

This is a concert poster design for Destroyer, a Canadian rock band from Vancouver, British Columbia, fronted by singer-songwriter Dan Bejar. Unlike their band name, their songs are sentimental and delicate. The album "Kaputt" contains not only very lonesome and melancholic moods but also retro, 80's elements in the music. The designer Jaemin Lee tried to reproduce an image of the 80's in this poster. The letters in the word "DESTROYER" is gathering in the darkness, and is made with rough polygons, texture patterns and two quiet colours which reminds him of the 80's era and faded memories.

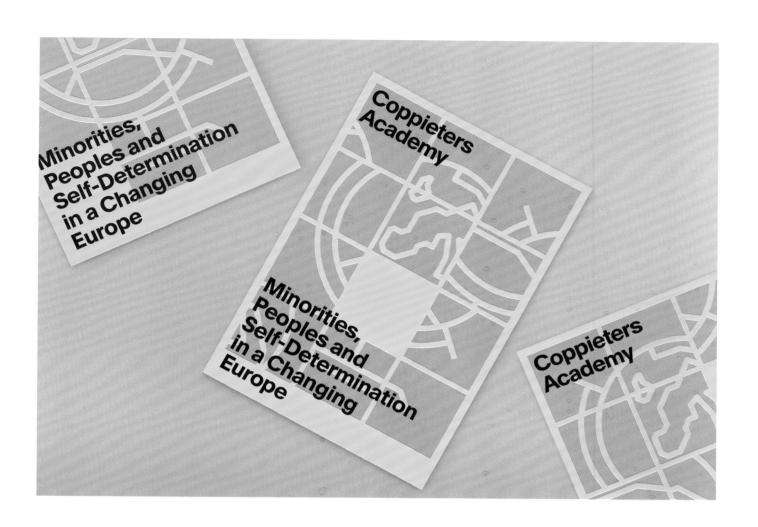

 C5 M15 Y100 K0 + C72 M12 Y10 K0

Coppieters Academy

Design Studio: Familia
Creative Director: Aleix Artigal
Designer: Aleix Artigal
Client: Coppieters Foundation

The Coppieters Academy is a three-day intensive study programme at the heart of Europe's political capital, Brussels. The Academy is run by Coppieters Foundation, in which participants gain an in-depth knowledge on the European Union through a series of lectures, interactive workshops and study visits.

Familia's graphic proposal aims to represent several concepts such as politics, university, pedagogy, open mind, fun, creativity, and optimistic future. It's also linked to the idea of changing Europe, and the ideas related to evolution and progress. The studio was interested in the idea of construction as a metaphor for explaining the Academy and the shared knowledge.

Tempo

Designer: Ledoux Mélissa

Tempo is a fictional project, a dance hall in Lille which would offer a great variety of dance classes. It would take place in an old building, very well-known in Lille: le Palais Rameaux. Dynamic, colourful and playful, Tempo's identity is designed to match young and heterogeneous audiences. The identity is inclined to promote the opening of the dance hall.

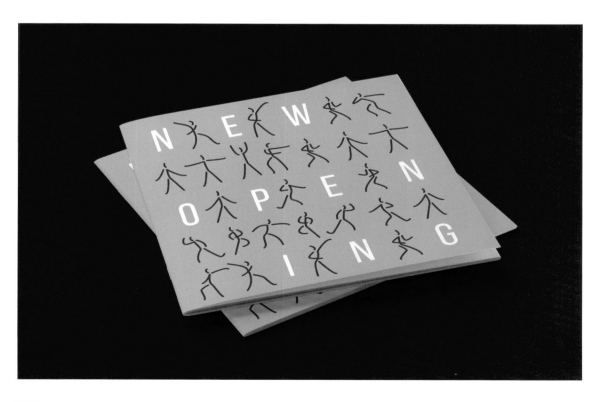

19.03.2018

NEW

OPENING

AU PALAIS RAMEAUX

WWW.TEMPO.FR

19.03.2018

NEW

OPEN

ING

AU PALAIS RAMEAUX

WWW.TEMPO.FR

 PANTONE 7488C + PANTONE Violet

Outlet Grandes Marcas

Design Studio: Oliver Digital
Creative Director: John Dias dos Santos
Designer: John Dias dos Santos
Client: Outlet Grandes Marcas

The project was carried out for a large garment outlet in Paraná, Brazil, where the agency Oliver Digital was responsible for the care, and the art director John Dias for the creation and concept of the visual identity. A background pattern was created and they used very vibrant colours to draw attention from the visitors of the outlet.

PANTONE 802 C + PANTONE 2755 C

R Cariri Gênese

Design Studio: Gruta Design
Creative Director: Felipe Kariri
Designers: Abel Alencar, Diogo Ribeiro, Felipe Kariri,
Helton Cardoso, Petroneo Fernandes, Rhuan Nauê,
Samuell Dias, Van Carvalho

R* Design – Cariri (12th *Regional meeting of
Design Students), an itinerant event of academic,
scientific and cultural nature, held annually in
different cities of Brazil.

The event raises "Gênese" (Genesis) that
symbolizes the search for a new vision of design
and its transformative role in the world. The Visual
Identity covers not only the beginning of the
design, but also the course of its evolution that is
related to man as the protagonist of his history,
a free being who seeks to tread in his footsteps
rummaging in his origins the way to liberation,
striking reflection of the Cariri region.

The colours represent the depth of design since its
origins trace your journey through time plunging
into its fantastic and enchanting universe, source
of light that illuminates new paths to follow. The
future is just a new beginning.

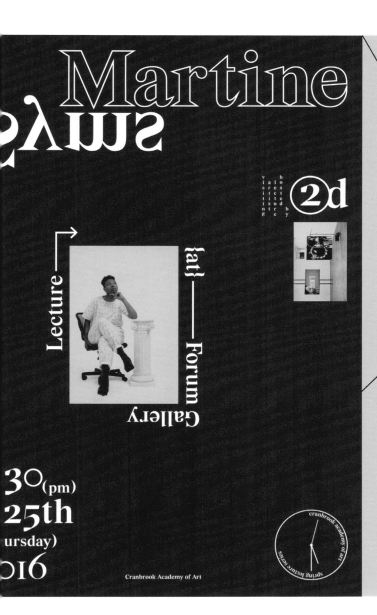

Martine Syms is an artist based in Los Angeles. She is the founder of **Dominica**, a publishing imprint dedicated to exploring blacknuss in visual culture. From 2007–11, Syms directed Golden Age, a proje̶c̶t̶ ̶b̶a̶sed on printed m̶a̶t̶e̶r̶i̶a̶l̶. work has been ex̶h̶i̶b̶i̶t̶e̶d̶ ̶screened extensively, including presentations at the New Museum, The Studio Museum in Harlem, Museum of Contemporary Art Los Angeles, MCA Chicago, Green Gallery, Gene Siskel Film Center, and White Flag Projects. She has lectured at Yale University, SXSW, California Institute of the Arts, University of Chicago, The Broad, Johns Hopkins University, and MoMA PS1, among other venues.

martinesyms.com

◗ R189 G232 B84 + R83 G22 B186

Martine Syms Lecture Poster

Designer: Qingyu Wu
Client: Cranbrook Academy of Art

Qingyu designed the poster for Martine Syms's lecture at Cranbrook Academy of Art Forum Gallery, which was held on February 25th, 2016.

The colour purple is a theme in artist and "conceptual entrepreneur" Martine Syms's work. The designer wanted to combine two intense colours to bring energy, stylish, and attention. This colour combination draws the audience to performer/ lecturer, stirs emotions and has a huge impact on identity recognition.

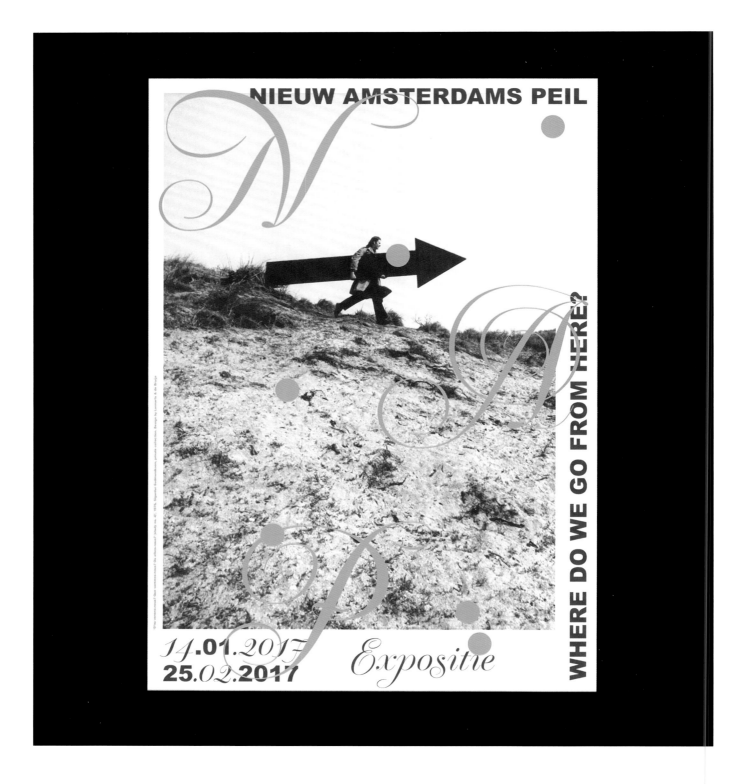

 PANTONE Violet U + PANTONE 3395 U

Nieuw Amsterdams Peil

Design Studio: Studio Lennarts & de Bruijn
Clients: Annet Gelink Gallery, Ellen de Bruijne Projects,
Galerie Fons Welters, Gallery Stigter van Doesburg,
tegenboschvanvreden, Martin van Zomeren

Amsterdam starts a bold new initiative where six of the premier galleries in the Jordaan—Annet Gelink Gallery, Ellen de Bruijne Projects, Galerie Fons Welters, Gallery Stigter van Doesburg, tegenboschvanvreden and Martin van Zomeren—come together to make one expanded exhibition, "Where do we go from here?" across all six galleries. The show was curated by Alessandro Vincentelli (BALTIC Centre for Contemporary Art). Lennarts & de Bruijn made a concept and visual identity for this new initiative, based on the galleries' locations in Amsterdam and the retro typography used back in the day.

NIEUW AMSTERDAMS PEIL

13.01.2017

WHERE DO WE GO FROM HERE?
SAVE THE DATE
Opening: Friday January 13, 17.00 – 20.00 hrs

Annet Gelink Gallery
Ellen de Bruijne Projects
Galerie Fons Welters
Galerie Stigter Van Doesburg
tegenboschvanvreden
Martin van Zomeren

Amsterdam is een bijzonder initiatief rijker: zes top-galeries in de Jordaan – Annet Gelink Gallery, Ellen de Bruijne Projects, Galerie Fons Welters, Galerie Stigter Van Doesburg, tegenboschvanvreden en Martin van Zomeren – organiseren samen een kunstproject onder de titel 'Where Do We Go From Here?' In een tijd waarin cultuur onder druk staat en waarin populisme hoogtij viert, is er grote behoefte aan een ander antwoord op versnippering, individualisme, eigenbelang en angst. De zes galeries functioneren voor dit project als één tentoonstellingsruimte waar werk te zien is van een selectie van ca. 22 kunstenaars, verspreid over de locaties. Ook de openbare ruimte tussen de galeries wordt meegenomen in het tentoonstellingsconcept.

'Where Do We Go From Here?' wil een positief initia-tief zijn, met speciaal voor deze gelegenheid gemaakte kunstwerken, waaronder performances en site-specific werk. De titel van de tentoonstelling is ontleend aan een werk van kunstenaar Sigurdur Gudmundsson, 'D'Oú Venons nous? Que Somme-nous? Où Allons-nous? (study no. 4)', uit 1976. De vraag in de titel suggereert de mogelijkheid van verandering. Het unieke evenement weerspiegelt de dynamiek van de kunstscène waar Amsterdam met recht trots op kan zijn.

13.01.2017 – 25.02.2017

NIEUW AMSTERDAMS PEIL

Amsterdam starts a bold new initiative where six of the premier galleries in the Jordaan – Annet Gelink Gallery, Ellen de Bruijne Projects, Galerie Fons Welters Gallery, Stigter van Doesburg, tegenboschvanvreden and Martin van Zomeren – come together to make one expanded exhibition, 'Where do we go from Here?' across all six galleries. At a time when culture is under pressure and that populism is rampant, there is great need for a different response to the fragmentation, individualism, self-interest and fear. For this project, the six galleries function as one exhibition space, where you can see work from a selection of 22 artists, across the loca-tions. The routes and the public space between the galleries form part of the exhibition concept.

'Where Do We Go From Here?' seeks to be a wholly positive initiative, with newly created artworks, inclu-ding performances and site-specific work. The title of the exhibition is taken from a work by artist Sigurdur Gudmundsson, 'D'oú Venons nous ? Que Somme-nous? Où Allons-nous? (study no.4)' from 1976. The question in the title suggests the possibility of change. This unique event reflects the dynamics of the art scene which Amsterdam can justly be so proud of.

Curator: Alessandro Vincentelli (BALTIC Centre for Contemporary Art). Producer: Imara Limon
Design: www.lennartsendebruijn.com

한국 건축의 다양성
Diversity of Korean Architecture
#1: 주식회사 종합건축사 설계사무소 - 박길룡
2017년 4월 19일 오후 7:30
forumnforum.com

한국 건축의 다양성
Diversity of Korean Architecture
#2: 중대형 (설계)사무소의 출현과 도심재개발사업 - 박정현
2017년 4월 26일 오후 7:30
forumnforum.com

From left to right

C20 M75 Y75 K0 + C75 M0 Y60 K0

C90 M90 Y10 K0 + C0 M80 Y85 K0

C85 M0 Y35 K0 + C40 M45 Y75 K15

C0 M90 Y35 K0 + C75 M0 Y75 K0

Diversity of Korean Architecture

Design Studio: studio fnt
Designer: Jaemin Lee
Client: Junglim Foundation

These are poster series for the forums held by Junglim Foundation, namely Diversity of Korean Architecture. The four-time forums dealt with various aspects of Korean modern architecture. Architecture is not led by several leading architects. Most buildings in Korea, that the citizens actually utilize on a day-to-day basis, do not go through enough thoughts and research processes in their making. This forum is an opportunity to look deep into the history of methodology and development process of large-scale architecture, such as office buildings, shopping centers, apartments, hospital and churches, designed not by famous "star architects" but ordinary design offices.

Studio fnt made four symbolic graphics which are reminiscent of traditional forms and colours of Korea, and represent the theme of each forum—general conditions and characteristics of Korean modern design firms, office buildings, residential premises and communities and religious architecture.

한국 건축의 다양성
Diversity of Korean Architecture
#3: 기록되지 않은 주거의 공간 - 정다은, 이인규
2017년 5월 10일 오후 7:30
forumnforum.com

한국 건축의 다양성
Diversity of Korean Architecture
#4: 1970년대 이후 한국 개신교 윤리와 교회건축 - 이은석
2017년 5월 17일 오후 7:30
forumnforum.com

 PANTONE 802 + PANTONE Dark Blue

PANTONE 267+ PANTONE 805

Catalunya Film Festivals

Design Studio: Familia
Creative Director: Aleix Artigal
Designer: Aleix Artigal
Client: Catalunya Film Festivals

Catalunya Film Festival is the association of film festivals, film and video presentations of Catalonia, Spain.

The logo and graphics system were developed based on the concepts of light and cinematographic focus. The formalisation of the graphic line is articulated through the repeated use of typography, the 30-degree inclination and the masking of the circle.

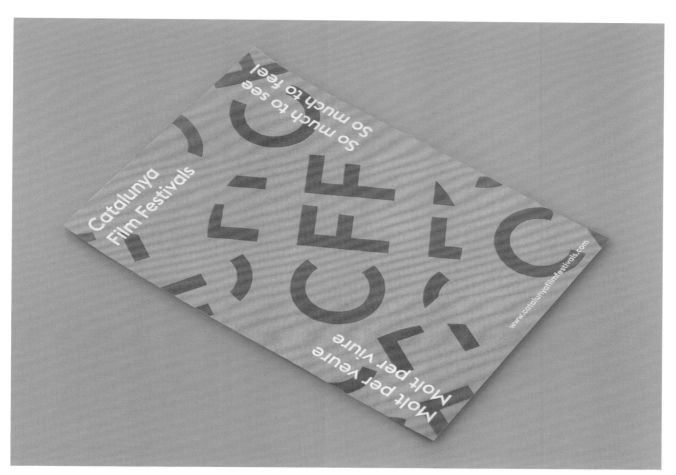

 PANTONE Blue 072 U + PANTONE 805 U

PANTONE Blue 072 U + PANTONE 810 U

PANTONE Blue 072 U + PANTONE 802 U

L'ETAGE

Design Studio: Le Jardin Graphique
Creative Director: Stéphanie Triballier
Designer: Stéphanie Triballier
Client: Citédia services

For two years, L' ETAGE, based in Rennes city, which is a music room for current and contemporary music, has developed a true graphical identity that became a collection throughout the seasons. First built as a mountain or a building, from floor to floor, the different letters compose and shape the artwork of the L' ETAGE. In addition, night and urban life scenes are superimposed on top of the letters. A theme, which reflects textures from the city, was added to the photographic material, such as scratched paper, lights, and graphs, etc.

L'ÉTAGE
LE LIBERTÉ

L'ÉT ÉTAGE

2017
2018

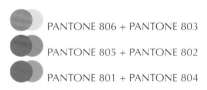

PANTONE 806 + PANTONE 803

PANTONE 805 + PANTONE 802

PANTONE 801 + PANTONE 804

Katowice Street Art Festival 2016

Designer: Marta Gawin
Client: Instytucja Kultury Katowice – Miasto Ogrodów

Going beyond Street Art – that was the main idea standing by 2016 edition of the Festival. The question of what actions in public space bring to the city, what value they add and whether they change anything at all will be more important than pondering whether or not these actions are still street art. Provocative question about the limits of street art was made by juxtaposing meticulously ornamented empty frames with simple typography.

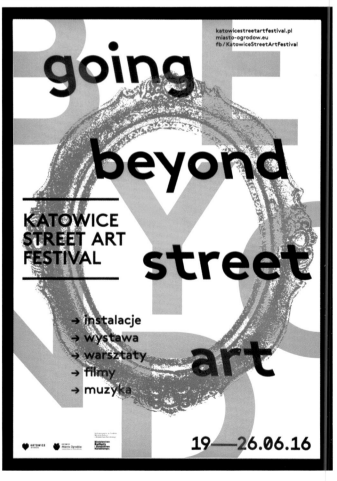

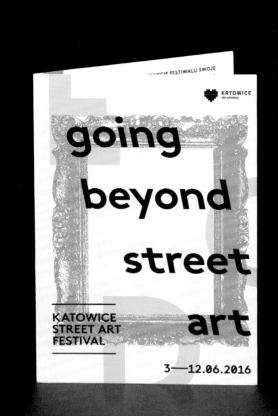

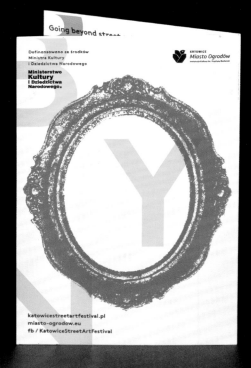

going beyond street art

KATOWICE
STREET ART
FESTIVAL

3—12.06.2016

katowicestreetartfestival.pl
miasto-ogrodow.eu
fb / KatowiceStreetArtFestival

Dofinansowano ze środków
Ministra Kultury
i Dziedzictwa Narodowego

Ministerstwo
Kultury
i Dziedzictwa
Narodowego.

KATOWICE
Miasto Ogrodów

Going beyond street art.

Już od pierwszej edycji festiwalowa formuła street artu mocno nas uwierała. Dzisiaj, po latach krytycznego patrzenia na zjawisko wiemy, że wymyka się ono prostym definicjom. Podczas tegorocznej edycji spróbujemy wyjść poza street art. Nie dlatego, że przestał być ważny, ale dlatego, żeby sprawdzić czy nie ma go gdzieś indziej. Istotniejsze od zastanawiania się nad tym czy robimy street art czy już nie, będzie pytanie o to, co nasze działania w przestrzeni publicznej dają miastu i jaką mają dla niego wartość. Wyjście poza street art na pewno nie da nam łatwych odpowiedzi, pozwoli jednak poszerzyć horyzont naszych poszukiwań.

Patroni medialni:

SZUM W M reflektor ultramaryna

Partnerzy:

KZGM Komunalny Zakład Gospodarki Mieszkaniowej w Katowicach · ZZM · MDK POŁUDNIE · Wydział Malarstwa i Nowych Mediów AKADEMIA SZTUKI W SZCZECINIE · BIURO DŹWIĘKU KATOWICE

KATOWICE STREET ART FESTIVAL
19—26.06.2016
_____

8—30.06
„25/7" DWA ZETA
Galeria Pusta, Miasto Ogrodów,
pl. Sejmu Śląskiego 2
Wernisaż: 8.06.2016, godz. 19.00
→ wystawa

19.06, godz. 14.00—18.00
BIURO DŹWIĘKU KATOWICE
+ BURNT FRIEDMANN LIVE
Muszla koncertowa, Park Bogucki
→ Popołudniowy Plener Dźwiękowy

21—25.06, godz. 15.00—18.00
OTWARTA PRACOWNIA VLEPKI
Prowadzenie: Kwiaciarnia Grafiki
ul. Stanisława 4
Strat pracowni: 21.06, godz. 19.00
→ warsztaty

22.06, godz. 18.00
„PIXADORES",
reż. Amir Escandari,
„LA COMUNA 9. ODZYSKUJĄC
MIASTO", reż. Inga Hajdarowicz,
Anna Bednarczyk
Drzwi Zwane Koniem,
ul. Warszawska 37
→ Pokazy filmowe
_____

26.06, godz. 15.00
PIKNIK NA KOSZUTCE
Pomnik Rodzina, pl. Grunwaldzki

W TRAKCIE FESTIWALU SWOJE PROJEKTY REALIZOWAĆ BĘDĄ:
_____

ŁUKASZ BERGER
więcej informacji na stronie internetowej festiwalu
_____

PRZEMEK KOPCZYK
projekt oparty na stronie www,
Katowice/Śląsk
_____

SZYMON PIETRASIEWICZ
dzielnica Murcki, Katowice
_____

SPOŁECZNA PRACOWNIA
MOZAIKI
Mozaika na Pomniku Rodzina,
pl. Grunwaldzki, Katowice
_____

JOANNA STEMBALSKA
ul. Kościuszki, Katowice
_____

SUPERGUT STUDIO
przestrzeń nad Rawą,
pomiędzy al. Korfantego 1 i 3,
Katowice
_____

MARIUSZ WARAS
I STUDENCI AKADEMII SZTUKI
W SZCZECINIE
ul. Górnicza 7, Katowice

February: Risograph Ink: Sunflower + Hunter Green

August: Risograph Ink: Fluorescent Pink + Federal Blue

April: Risograph Ink: Aqua + Black

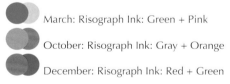
March: Risograph Ink: Green + Pink

October: Risograph Ink: Gray + Orange

December: Risograph Ink: Red + Green

2018 Calendar

Design Studio: Studio OYE / *Creative Director:* O Hezin / *Designer:* O Hezin

Calendars have limited numbers and letters, but even so, with only one initial letter, people know very well what it means. For example, if people just look at the first page "J", they realize that it is January. The designer was interested in that point and thought about how to extend the graphic with limited letters, which reminded her of word cards.

Instead of presenting words from "A to Z" in alphabetical order, the designer listed words according to corresponding months. Among the numerous English vocabularies, she has chosen very easy words that are obvious to everyone, which could be clearly expressed through illustrations. As the calendar usually requires two colours to distinguish between weekdays and weekends, the designer played with the Risograph ink to create 12 duotone graphics.

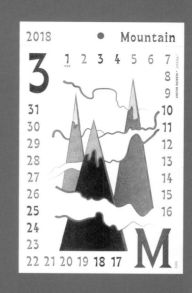

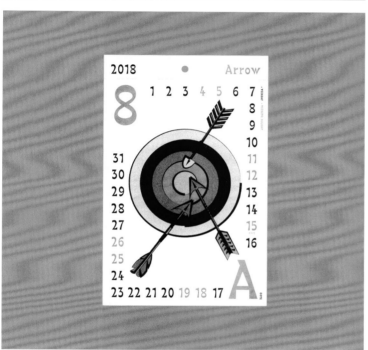

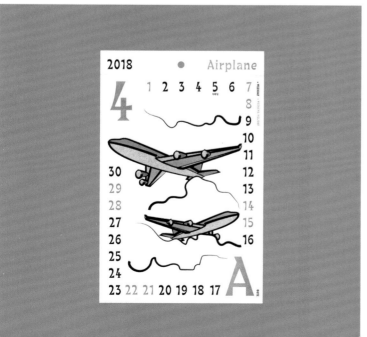

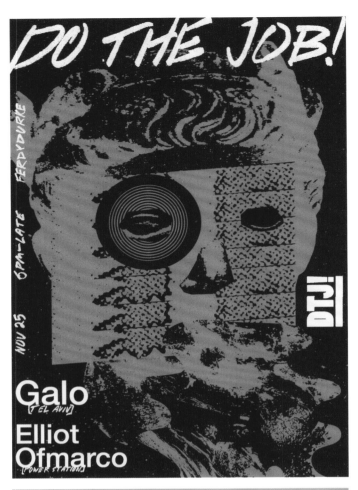

C0 M84 Y74 K0 + C69 M95 Y6 K32

C0 M22 Y98 K0 + C0 M84 Y89 K3

C93 M10 Y20 K0 + C0 M76 Y64 K0

C0 M56 Y0 K56 + C86 M77 Y6 K0

Posters by Brodie Kaman

Designer: Brodie Kaman
Clients: Outer Body, Do The Job

These posters were made by graphic designer Brodie Kaman during 2016 to 2017. His inspiration came from the artwork of the late 70s and early 80s punk movement. "With posters I like to take an experimental approach, seeking to make each one unique, playful and strong. I don't like to take too much time concepting with posters, but enjoy scribbling, looking through books and then doing some trial and error to achieve the desired look," Brodie says.

OUTER BODY

Friday June 17

"...an experience."

LUCA LOZANO

(Klasse/Sex Tags/UK)

Connections Nightclub

Hugo Gerani, Jack Dutrac, Mike Midnight, DJ Super Foreign, Lightsteed, Viv G, Louise B, Dj Hame & Willy Slade

TOM MOORE (OTOLOGIC)

(Animals Dancing/Melb)

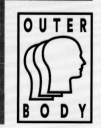

OUTER BODY

Duotone
Effects

1+1>2

 Risograph Ink: Bright Red U +
Medium Blue 286 U

Nikola Tesla / Pressbook

Designer: Mercedes Bazan

"Nikola Tesla / Pressbook" is a personal project of designer Mercedes Bazan. The intention was to explore Nikola Tesla's thoughts about energy. The colour of red represents the earth and the idea of terrene, whereas blue stands for spiritual energy. Risograph technique allows transparency and the blending of colours, which reinforced the concept of the two energies.

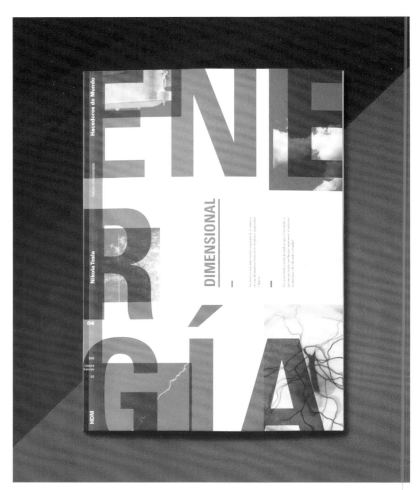

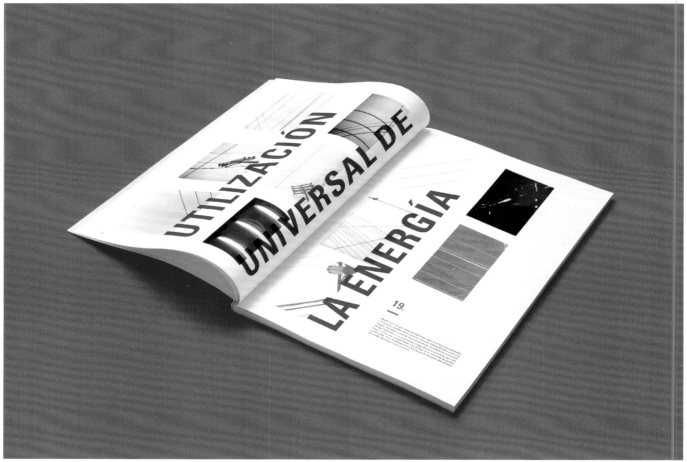

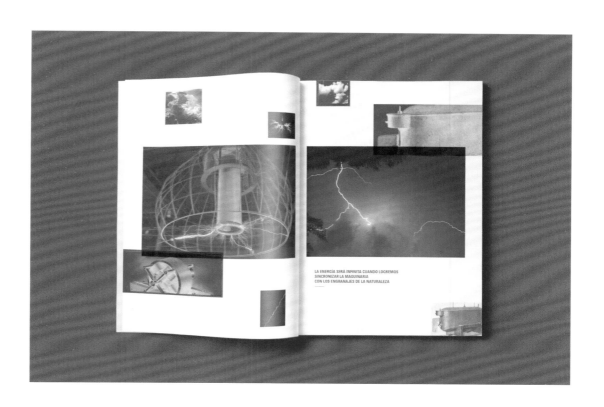

LA ENERGÍA SERÁ INFINITA CUANDO LOGREMOS
SINCRONIZAR LA MAQUINARIA
CON LOS ENGRANAJES DE LA NATURALEZA

Open City Documentary Festival Branding and Identity

Design Studio: Moving Studio
Creative Directors: Brett Wilkinson, Tom Saunders
Designers: Brett Wilkinson, Joe Small
Client: Open City Documentary Festival

Open City Documentary Festival (OCDF) is one of the UK's biggest film festivals dedicated solely to the art of documentary film making. Moving Studio designed the identity for the Festival's 2015 season, and they were invited again to design the 2016 festival with new campaign graphics. The festival needed to team up their new identity with a theme that would attract the attention of potential visitors, whilst raising the profile of the festival in London.

Building on the 2015 concept of space and community, 2016's aesthetic took a new direction, with the introduction of a second brand colour. Using colour graded images and dynamic new layouts, Moving Studio created a 40 page festival programme, posters, flyers and digital presentations. The 2016 festival was once again well attended and well received by film enthusiasts and industry professionals, keeping Open City at the forefront of documentary festivals in the UK.

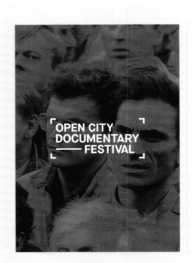

opencitylondon.com

Bringing the best of international documentary to London

facebook.com/opencitylondon — @opencitydocs

facebook.com/opencitylondon — @opencitydocs

OPEN CITY DOCUMENTARY —— FESTIVAL

21—26 June 2016

Picturehouse Central + JW3 + Regent Street Cinema + ICA
Bertha DocHouse + Hackney Picturehouse + Picturehouse Crouch End

UCL

 C100 M80 Y40 K60 + C0 M91 Y87 K0

MFB Annual Report 2016/2017

Design Studio: Vetro Design
Creative Director: Vince Aloi
Designer: Alexandar Darkovski
Client: Melbourne Fire Brigade

The concept for the 2017 MFB Annual Report is titled Future Forward. The MFB (Metropolitan Fire Brigade) aims to provide a world class fire and emergency service for citizens of Melbourne and Victoria and responds to hundreds of life-threatening emergencies per year.

The design concept represents an organisation in a current state of change, looking to the future and beyond, while also reflects on its key achievements over the past financial year. The use of bold colours, high-contrast duotones and minimalist typography symbolises the momentum and intensity of the emergencies coupled with the commitment by the firefighters to protect and save lives.

We are proud of our people and we will continue to invest in developing their skills and capabilities

Our priority is ensuring that everyone always returns home safe from work

We will work seamlessly with our partners to achieve the best outcomes for the community

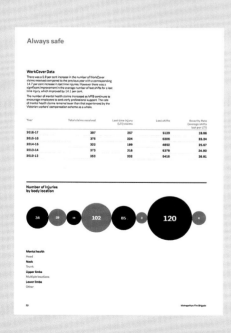

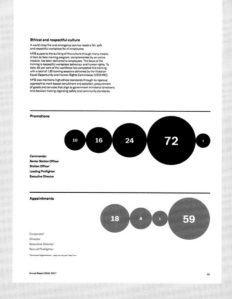

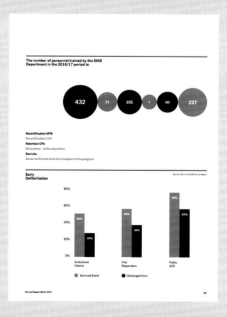

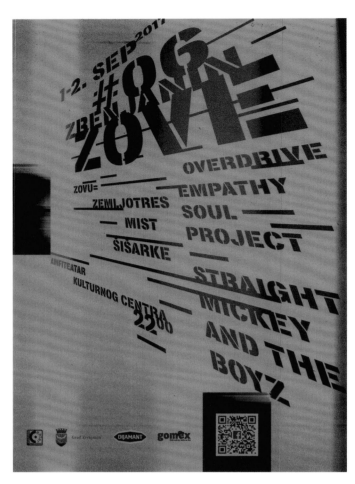

 C96 M100 Y26 K33 + C0 M78 Y93 K0

Zrenjanin Zove – Two Day Festival of Alternative Music

Design Studio: KulturKick Creative Productions
Creative Director: Vladimir Garboš
Designer: Vladimir Garboš
Client: Cultural Centre of Zrenjanin, Serbia

Zrenjanin Zove (Zrenjanin Calling) is a small two-day music festival in Zrenjanin, Serbia. With vol. 6, it became very important for young people and alternative and rock music scene. During 90's, town was renowned for this type of music and culture in whole. But with drastic decay in the beginning of 00's, only this festival endures with the idea of new music, underground culture and good music. So all this translates into concept and the approach on how to promote such not-so-profitable music scene and culture. With abundance of new techniques and possibilities, nice stock photos available, saturated market oriented promotional campaigns, the best way was not to do it like that at all, but to bring attention to how it was "in the golden age" of this scene. With small amounts of posters, billboards and stickers, this approach proved to be a hit! Besides the nice visual appeal, the reason for using these colour was that orange was the colour of seats in main auditorium of Cultural Centre, by which it was very recognizable and that dark blue is a kind of reference to something noble and exquisite.

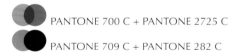

PANTONE 700 C + PANTONE 2725 C

PANTONE 709 C + PANTONE 282 C

Vênus

Designer: Mariana Gabardo
Mentor: Andréa Capra Galina

Vênus is a fictional film festival aimed at celebrating and supporting the work of women filmmakers and creatives across the crafts. With the purpose of promoting and praising the women's role in cinema, this project intends to increase visibility for female filmmakers and films with interesting and complex female characters.

The main concept was to create a flexible, cohesive and bold brand identity. The visual identity system made use of colours and duotone effect which were essentials to create a uniform and contemporary communication.

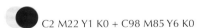

C2 M22 Y1 K0 + C98 M85 Y6 K0

New York Women's Surf Film Festival

Designer: Shanti Sparrow
Client: Lava Girl Surf

The New York Women's Surf Film Festival, a project of Lava Girl Surf, celebrates the filmmakers and female wave riders who live to surf, highlighting their sense of adventure, connection to the ocean and love for their own communities and those they discover. The branding design for the 5th annual film festival was influenced by iconic retro surf culture and the nuanced aesthetics of contemporary film. The incredible underwater photography of Sarah Lee has been augmented with nostalgic sunset colours. The removal of contextual colours helped create an illusion whereby the surfer appears to be both swimming and flying. This visual double meaning is reflective of the empowering and aspirational themes of the film festival itself.

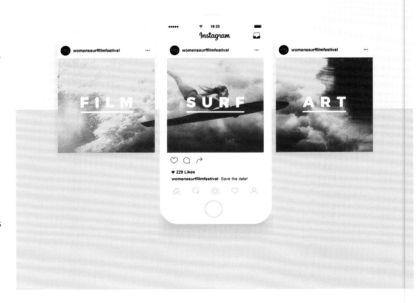

Corporate Design KunstSalon

Design Studio: Formdusche
Creative Directors: Svenja von Döhlen, Tim Finke,
Timo Hummel, Steffen Wierer
Designers: Svenja Eisenbraun, Lisa Stöckel
Client: Kunstsalon Cologne

As a private initiative for the promotion of art and culture, the
KunstSalon has pursued the goal of conveying the importance
of art and the need for its promotion since 1994.

The uniqueness of the KunstSalon lies in its multi-disciplinary
orientation: fine arts, drama, literature, music, dance, film – in
all areas, it acts as a promoter and mediator of art and culture.
As part of the redesign of the traditional brand, Formdusche
recreated the logo, which opens up a flexible space that
is filled with content. This corresponds to the idea of the
KunstSalon, which offers space, stage and screen for various
art forms.

In order to address a younger audience, the former wine
red has been changed to a more modern, bright red,
complemented with a progressive blue and a clear typography.

 PANTONE Blue 072 U + PANTONE 709 U

Roturas e Ligamentos

Designer: Dulce Cruz / *Illustrator:* André da Loba
Poet: Rita Taborda Duarte / *Photographer:* Sílvio Teixeira
Publisher: Abysmo / *Printer:* Orgal Impressores

To represent the title "Fractures and Ligaments", designer and illustrator have created a special book, making two different books connected by the back cover, allowing the reader to "break" and "re-attach" the illustrations to the text.

This book is paperback, with the content printed in one colour, and cover printed in two colours, on 150g Antalis Print Speed paper. The tinted edge symbolizes the fracture of the body when separating the two parts. The exposed binding allows a complete spread of the book pages so the reader can combine any poem with any illustration through an endless exploratory reading process. Left sided book is solely made of texts and has no images (except the cover), right side of the book is only made of drawings, even the bar code was cut to fit this rule.

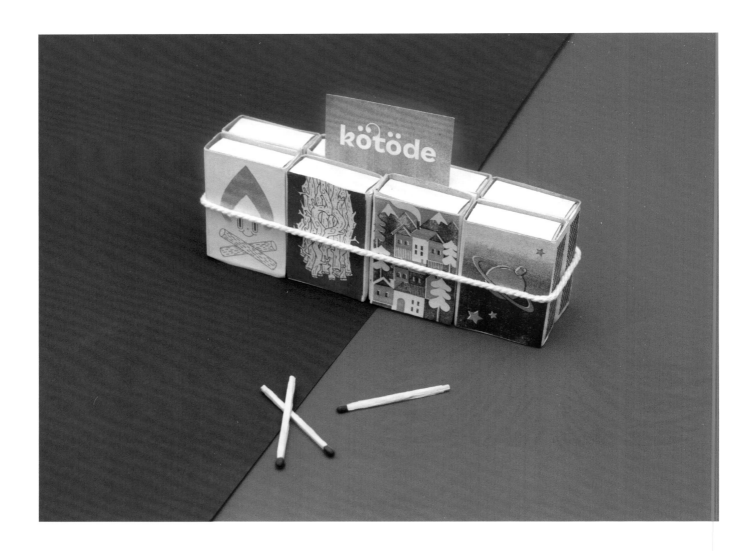

 Risograph Ink: Blue + Pink

Christmas Matches
and Postcards

Design Studio: Kötöde
Designers: Andrea Szabó, Dániel Bozzai, Dániel Máté, Fruzsina Foltin, Júlia Nizák, Ivett Lénárt, Réka Imre, Tamás Boldizsár Hoffmann

The group Kötöde designed a special Christmas themed series of matchboxes for the Holidays. All packs contain eight different matchboxes, each with a unique print on the top. On the back of the paper boxes, one can find the greetings from the group. The collection of the graphics was also published as postcards on white Munken paper. The whole project was printed with Risograph technology with pink and blue ink.

Risograph Ink:
Fluorescent Orange + Blue

Anátema

Designer: Heitor Kimura
Risograph Printing: Meli-Melo Press
Launched by Olho Vivo Publicações
Independentes at Feira Plana 2015

Anátema (Anathema) is a zine with visual
compositions inspired by philosophical
concepts and their creators. This issue features
the following philosophers: Socrates, Aristotle,
Parmenides, Plato, Nietzsche, Berkeley, Kant,
Spinoza, Deleuze, Parnet and Jean-Paul Sartre.

Anathema is a term derived from Greek
"something dedicated" and, in the Septuagint
and New Testament, it means "something
dedicated to evil and thus accursed".

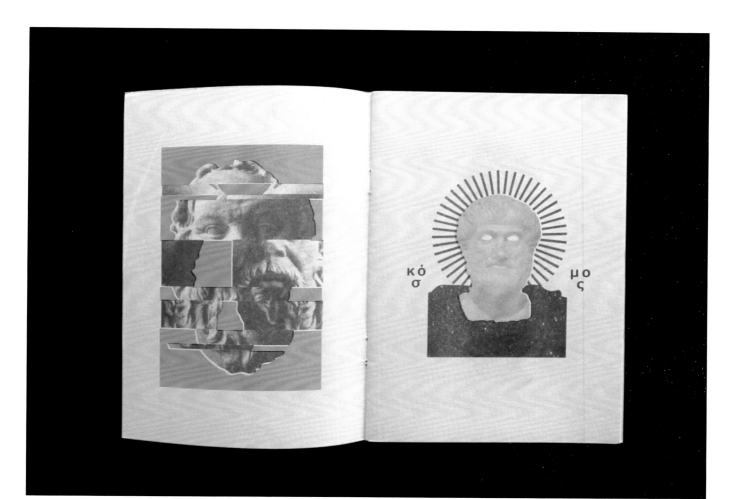

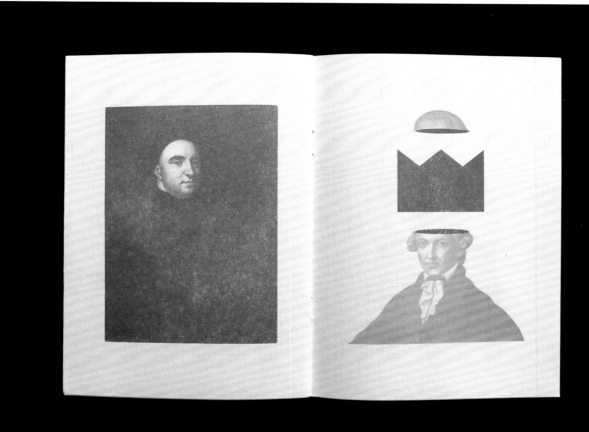

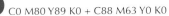
Compagnia Teatrale Nino Martoglio
2017/2018

Design Studio: K95
Creative Director: Danilo De Marco
Designers: Dario Leonardi, Danilo De Marco, Marco Giannì
Copywriter: Federica Musumeci
Client: Compagnia Teatrale Nino Martoglio

The Nino Martoglio's theatrical company is a troupe of actors from Catania, Italy, who play both dramatic and comic performances. Design studio K95 created the company's new visual identity for the 2017/2018 season. In the logo, the image of the face has been vectorized and the MN monogram was placed inside a circle. For the theatrical season identity, K95 used illustrations which represent the different theatrical plays. They overlapped geometrical shapes, such as circle and rectangle, to these illustrations, in order to convey the information about the four theatrical plays.

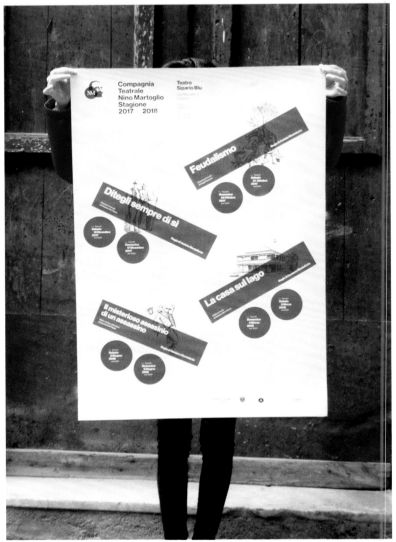

Wayward Arts Magazine

Design Studio: Blok Design
Creative Directors: Vanessa Eckstein, Marta Cutler
Designers: Vanessa Eckstein, Kevin Boothe, Miki Arai
Collaborator: Dr. Bob Deutsch
Client: Wayward Arts Magazine

This is Blok Design's editorial design project for Wayward Arts, a non-profit magazine in support of Canada's design and arts community. The theme of this issue is called counterculture. To put a sharper lens on this vast subject, Blok Design collaborated with Dr. Bob Deutsch, noted cultural anthropologist, who also contributed an essay. The issue is a celebration of what happens when art, politics and design come together to change history, and an expression of the belief that design is at its best when it serves society.

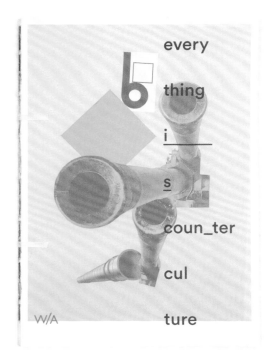

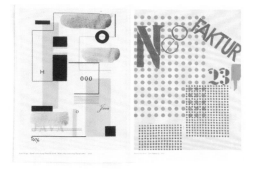

Black Power Salute at Olympic Games / Mexico City / 1968   Ferguson Solidarity March / New York / 2014   Tahrir Square / Egypt / 2011

Nelson Mandela / South Africa / 1994   Eustachy Kossakowski / Tadeusz Kantor / Panoramic Sea Happening / 1967

C73 M28 Y0 K6 + Pink paper colour

Earthquake Fanzine

Designer: Marisol De la Rosa Lizárraga

An earthquake with an estimated magnitude of 7.1 occurred in Central Mexico, on September 19, 2017. The same thing occurred 32 years ago, on the same day.

"The memories of the 1985 earthquake were part of a story I would never imagine to experience just like my parents did during their youth," says Marisol, the designer of the fanzine, "Even though I was a witness through the television screen and social media, myself as a Mexican can't help to feel touched about the whole incidents. Mexico suffered twice on the same day but with a huge contrast on how information spread."

The title is attributed to Gustavo Cerati's song of the same name. This fanzine gathers the most outstanding events the weeks after the earthquake. The chosen colour palette has the purpose of giving a melancholic and nostalgic feeling, rather than the chaotic and aggressive design of the popular Mexican fanzine style.

Y SE DISCULPARON

> NOS LLEVÓ A LA CONCLUSIÓN DE QUE EN CASO DE HABER UN SOBRE-VIVIENTE, NO NECE-SARIAMENTE ES UNA MENOR DE EDAD.

El almirante Ángel Enrique Sarmiento, sub secretario de Marina, se disculpó esta noche por el caso Frida Sofía.

16   17

El grupo no recibe retribución de ningún tipo, ni de parte de autoridades nacionales o locales, y se man tienen con donaciones.

24

Aesthetics & Typography

Designer: Lucia Rossetti

Aesthetics & Typography is a personal project of designer Lucia Rossetti. For six consecutive weeks, she read, discussed and dissected six critical texts relating to aesthetics and the subjectivity of taste. After reading and understanding the texts, she visually responded to the pieces, focusing on how typography could carry a message or a concept. She chose to print her responses out in bright pink and royal blue simply because they are her favorite colours and she wanted the publication to showcase her particular style and personal taste.

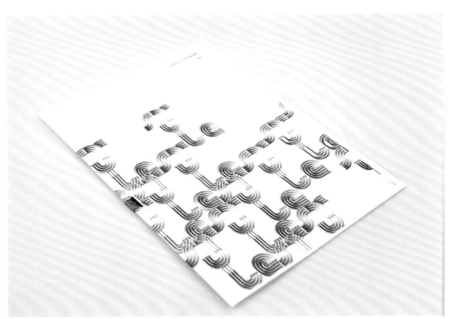

Risograph Ink: Fluorescent Pink + Blue

Pet Toy DIY

Design Studio: J.H.Graphic Studio / *Creative Director:* Jihye Kim / *Designer:* Jihye Kim

This Risograph project made by Designer Jihye Kim is an interesting guidebook for people with dogs. It introduces how they could use recycled products to make toy for the puppy.

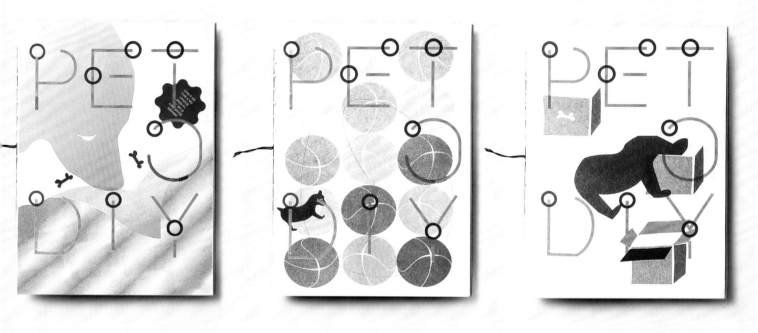

Alfabeto Plomo71

Design Studio: Coletivo Plomo71
Designers: Alice Neumann, Ana Laydner,
Henrique Beier, Sauê Ferlauto

Coletivo Plomo71 is a collaboration between four designers who share the same interest in typography. Their project "Alphabet" contains 36 characters, including letters and numbers. Each member of the studio was responsible for the design of nine characters, without knowing the characters chosen by their colleagues. These characters were vectorized and organized in Glyphs in the poster, which was then sent to print in Risograph. Fluorescent pink and blue ink were chosen because these colours are complementary to each other. The contrast between the fluorescent pink and darker blue makes it highly visible from far away while it also allows the details to be observed on a closer inspection by the viewer.

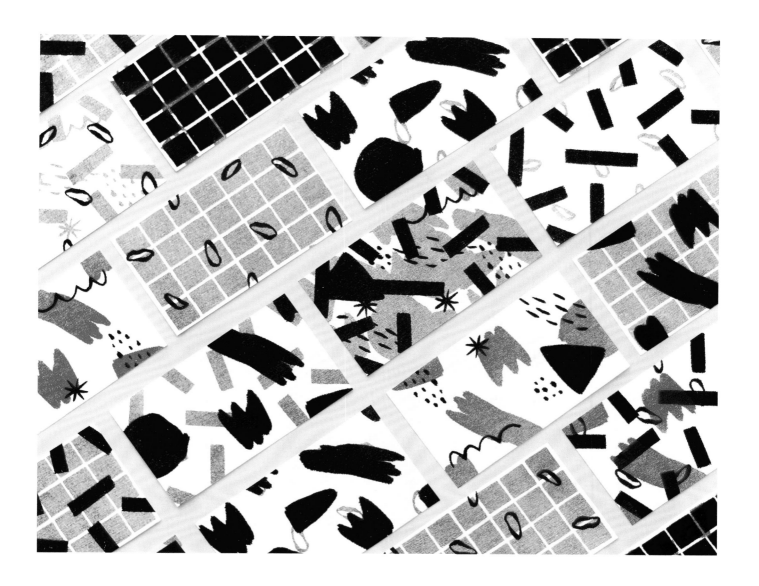

 Risograph Ink: Federal Blue + Fluorescent Pink

Personal Business Cards

Designer: Marina Cardoso

The project came up with an intention of developing personal business cards that could be playful and catchy. After various sketches and tests on graphic elements, many components such as stains, lines, drips and glitches were picked to compose different patterns. The idea of abstract patterns and illustrations seemed to match nicely the imperfect textures of Risograph printing. The overlaying possibilities of the printing technique added up with the abstract-organic aspects of the project and the strong pink and blue Risograph colour combination. The result is a dozen design variants combination, which makes each card unique in the overall series.

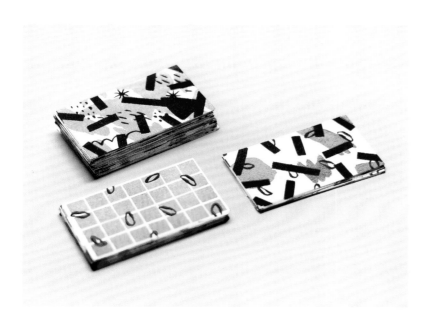

Fade to Blue

Design Studio: Onion Design Associates
Creative Director: Andrew Wong
Designers: Karen Tsai, Andrew Wong
Client: Tree Music Ltd.

Chung Yufeng, a pipa (Chinese lute) player, and David Chen, a U.S. born blues guitarist, combined the unlikely sounds of pipa and blues guitar in a collaborative music project called "Fade to Blue". The CD is a live recording consisting of only two instruments, a Chinese pipa and an acoustic blues guitar with no other backing instrument. It is a dialogue between two musicians and two instruments, between the East and the West, a man and a woman from different cultural and musical backgrounds. In order to capture the purity of their collaboration, only two colours were used on the entire album. Red ink for the pipa, the female musician, the East. While blue ink represented the blues guitar, the male and also all the English text he wrote. Letterpress printing was also used to reinforce raw and organic nature of their performance.

PANTONE 877 C + PANTONE 805 C

PANTONE 877 C + PANTONE 801 C

Cult Film Festival 2016

Design Studio: Tomorrow Design Office
Creative Director: Ray L.
Illustrator: Li Chi Tak
Client: Film Culture Centre, Hong Kong

Cult Film Festival 2016 was dedicated to the discovery and re-imagination of "CULT"! It showcased eight films celebrating the unique voices from every genre in the film world.

The key visual identity was centred on "Cult"– a way to disregard the grid system, traditional design method and logic by placing various elements randomly to become a visual venture into the uncompromising creative minds.

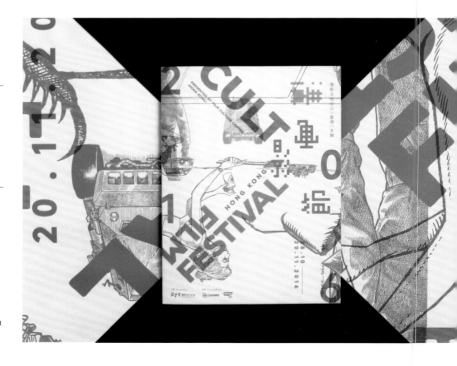

 PANTONE 172 C + PANTONE 285 C

En caisse

Design Studio: Les produits de l'épicerie
Creative Director: Jérôme Grimbert
Designer: Jérôme Grimbert
Client: Cie Théâtre du prisme (Theater Company – Lille France)

The idea of the visual was to represent the cashier by erasing her face with the bar code. She is no longer a person, and she becomes the product sold in the supermarket, passed on the treadmills of her cash register. The design studio chose to work on two colours in order to strengthen the impact and simplicity of the image.

 Risograph Ink: Medium Blue + Fluorescent Orange

Glasgow Alphabet

Designer: Marine Laurent
Printing: Risotto Studio

This Glasgow Alphabet is a personal illustrative project of Marine Laurent. The idea for this poster was to present the city of Glasgow, Scotland by using words and pictures. Each letter of the alphabet is associated to a word and an illustration related to the Scottish city. This alphabet illustrates the personal vision that Marine Laurent had of the city.

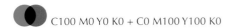 C100 M0 Y0 K0 + C0 M100 Y100 K0

Not Official San Valentino 2016

Design Studio: Bocanegra Studio
Creative Directors: Roberto Sensi, Sara Marigliani
Designers: Roberto Sensi, Sara Marigliani
Client: Umbria Music Commission

Not Official San Valentino is a festival that takes place every year in Terni, Italy, around Valentine's Day. During that period in the city, there was a rich program of events, so NOSV needs a breaking identity according to its nature of independent festival, already emphasized by the intentionally incorrect name.

The logo summarizes the concept: one person's meeting with another person (in love, in friendship, in arts, in family) makes something new and more powerful. Two symbols, people and hearts, when combined together create a new one. The two colours, red and cyan, in overprint make a third colour black. The designers rasterized the images and icons using parts of the logo, like hearts and circle.

TEATRO G.MANINI NARNI

Tickets

Singolo evento

PLATEA € 15,00
PALCHI € 13,00
LOGGIONE € 11,50

Abbonamento

PLATEA € 35,00
PALCHI € 32,00
LOGGIONE € 28,00

TEATRO G.MANINI
Via Giuseppe Garibaldi 29
Narni
T 0744 726362

PUNTI VENDITA AUTORIZZATI:

NEW SINFONY
Galleria del Corso 12
Terni
T 895 9697911

ALDO ALDINI
12 feb 21.30

Si avvicina alla magia da giovanissimo, complice il padre, illusionista ed escapologo a livello internazionale. Nel 2000 sviluppe le tecniche di mentalismo che lo portano, primo in Italia, all'attenzione del grande pubblico arrivando in finale ad Italia's Got Talent. L'illusionismo unito al mentalismo, gli permettono di dar vita ad esperimenti che hanno dell'incredibile, creando un fortissimo legame con il pubblico. Dopo aver incantato migliaia di spettatori in tutto il mondo, si esibirà a Narni con lo spettacolo "Sesto Senso" accompagnato al batterista Alexander Gentili.

MARCO MORANDI
20 feb 21.30

Figlio di Gianni, presenterà un viaggio musicale nella sua vita artistica e personale, dall'infanzia costantemente "sotto i riflettori", all'elaborazione della "condizione" di figlio d'arte, arrivando ai suoi primi 40 anni. Attraverso aneddoti e brani di autori conosciuti personalmente che hanno fatto la storia della musica e diventati per lui riferimenti, come Giorgio Gaber, Rino Gaetano e Lucio Dalla, suonerà dal vivo con una band di tre elementi. Con un'attenzione particolare ad alcuni storici pezzi del padre che, a suo modo, prenderà parte allo spettacolo.

LEVANTE
25 feb 21.30

Comincia a scrivere le prime canzoni a nove anni. Nel 2013, con "Alfonso", il suo grido disperato e ironico che recita "Che vita di merda" diventa il tormentone dell'estate. Nel 2015, dopo una tour americano, pubblica "Ciao per sempre". Il fortunato singolo anticipa l'uscita dell'album "Abbi cura di te", che la scorsa estate l'ha portata con grande successo in concerto in oltre 30 città italiane. In "Finché morte non ci separi" svela la struggente storia d'amore dei suoi genitori e canta accompagnata dalla madre, presente anche nell'incantevole videoclip.

VAL NOSV TABARD INN

la musica continuerà nello storico Pub Tabard In a metà stroda tra Terni

g Cats"

è una scuola di ballo swing che organizza corsi, festival, workshop e stage di li ed eventi mirati alla diffusione e alla promozione della cultura swing.

Minati"

o Gaetano, dopo aver girovagato in lungo e in largo per l'Italia con la Rino Gae-
a di intraprendere un percorso autonomo sempre all'insegna delle note graffianti e
de Rino.

"

segue in versione acustica brani degli anni 80. Ci farà assaporare i successi di
ckson, The Police, a-ha, Duran Duran, Simply Red, David Bowie e tanti altri.

Inizio spettacolo ore 23.30

o, presentando il voucher che trovi sul sito del NOSV, avrai diritto al 10%

notofficialsanvalentino/dopofestival

06, Narni.   **Tabard Inn**

o donne originarie del territorio narnese, che realizzano prodotti
ndo anche tecniche di ricamo antico. Durante i weekend del NOSV, nei
nno un mercatino artigianale animato da personaggi fantastici a cura
rifone".

ali a "L. di Fino" per i locali.

L. Di Fino
1923

NOT
OFFICIAL
SAN
VALENTINO

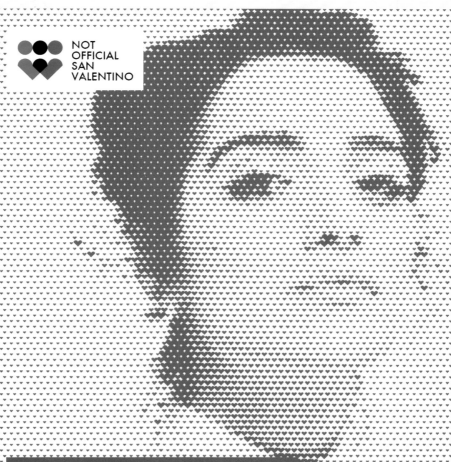

LEVANTE
25 feb 21.30
Teatro G. Manini Narni

NOT
OFFICIAL
SAN
VALENTINO

LEVANTE

25 feb 21.30

Teatro G. Manini Narni

NOT
OFFICIAL
SAN
VALENTINO

ALDO

12 feb 21

Teatro G. Manini

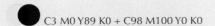

C3 M0 Y89 K0 + C98 M100 Y0 K0

Ordinary House

Design Studio: Brand Unit
Creative Director: Ulrike Tschabitzer-Handler
Art Director: Albert Handler
Graphic Designer: Zachary Kutz
Account Director: Andreas Oberkanins
Project Manager: Mandana Tischeh
Shop Designer: Claudia Cavallar
Client: McArthur Glen Designer Outlet Parndorf

Austrian designer Arnold Haas, who has been successfully operating his label WUBET for 10 years, runs the shop Ordinary House in Parndorf. The selection chosen by Haas unites the most outstanding representatives of the domestic fashion scene with the most interesting items from jewelry, product and furniture design and thus offers a "best-of" of the Austrian creative industry.

Brand unit designed the entire project for the second time for the McArthur Glen Designer Outlet Parndorf, including the communication design for the shop. Architect Claudia Cavallar planned the interior design, drawing on "Ready Mades". The furniture collection "Interioe", designed by Interio owner Janet Kath and the director of the Vienna Design Week Lilli Hollein in Austria and produced by local producers, formed the shop design for the Ordinary House.

AUSTRIAN DESIGN POP UP STORE

ORDINARY HOUSE

EQUIPPED BY
interio
Lebe glücklich. Lebe Design.

ab **11.04.2017**
McArthurGlen Designer Outlet Parndorf

... SAID THE FOX	PREGENZER
ADELINE GERMAIN	RANI BAGERIA
BATLINER	RIESS BY DOTTINGS
BRANDMAIR	RIVIVI 6269
CONSUMED BY THOMAS ZEITLBERGER	ROBERT HORN
EVA BLUT	ROBERT LA ROCHE
GOODGOODS	RUDOLF
INTERIOE	SAINT CHARLES APOTHEKE
KLEMENS SCHILLINGER	SIGHTLINE
LIA WOLF	SPIRIT OF OIL
LISKA	STUDIO DAVID TAVCAR
MARGARET AND HERMIONE	SUSA KREUZBERGER
MARK BAIGENT	SZIGETI
MEGUMI ITO	TEN DIZZY FINGERS
MODUS VIVENDI	THERMALBAD VÖSLAU KOLLEKTION
PETAR PETROV	TIME 4 AFRICA
PETRA HAUSER	VERONICA DREYER
PIA BAUERNBERGER	VANDASYE
	VOSSEN
	WUBET

DESIGNERS

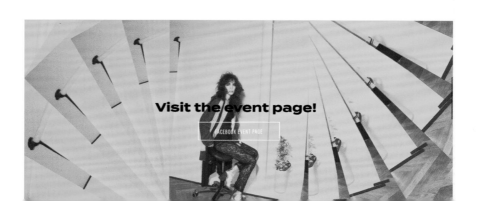

Visit the event page!

FACEBOOK EVENT PAGE

Risograph Ink: Warm Red U + Yellow U

Risograph Ink: Medium Blue 286 U + Yellow U

Lineage

Designers: Curtis Rayment, James Aspey, Alice Kumagami,
Aisling Sam, Lowena Hoskin
Client: India Lawton / British Art Show 8

The designers were assigned to produce a publication and poster for India Lawton's Lineage for the touring exhibition, British Art Show 8. The colour scheme was informed by the fluorescent colours. To achieve this, the designers used an in-house Risograph machine to explore and achieve exciting colour palettes to champion the rich photographs supplied by India Lawton.

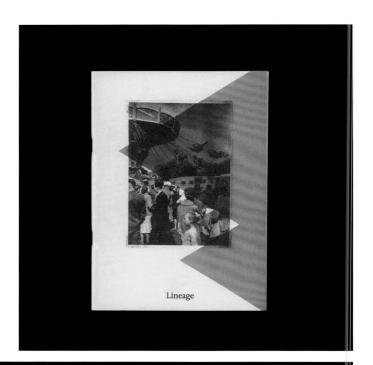

● Risograph Ink: Blue + Black

● Risograph Ink: Yellow + Black

● Risograph Ink: Purple + Black

● Risograph Ink: Red + Black

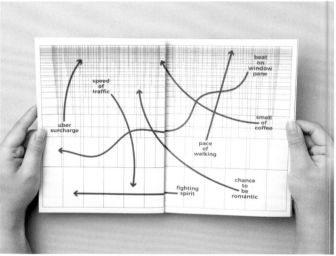

être, issues n°. 1-4

Design Studio: qu'est-ce que c'est design
Creative Director: Bryan Angelo Lim
Designers: Lim Jia Qing, Victoria Lee, Deborah Neo

"Être" is a French irregular verb which means "to be". It would conjugate differently when used in different contexts and voices. Each issue of the zine featured submissions from studio members, both permanent and transitory, and invited submissions, permitting the zine to present the many stories, interpretations and expressions that could emanate from one theme. The themes for the issue were something that people often overlook in their daily lives: rain, corner, breath and light, which were derived from the classical elements of water, earth, air and fire.

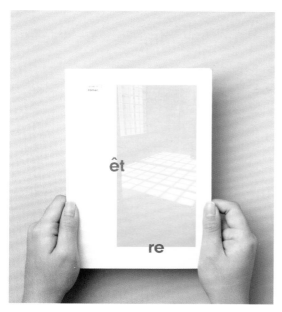

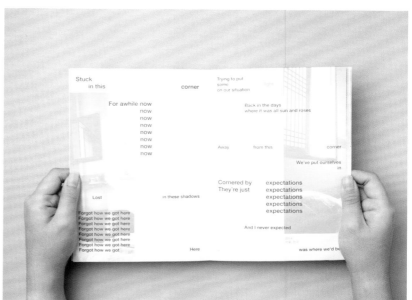

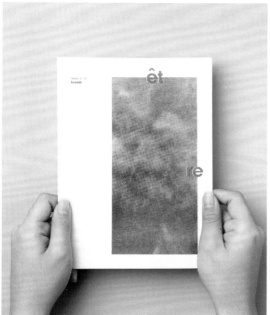

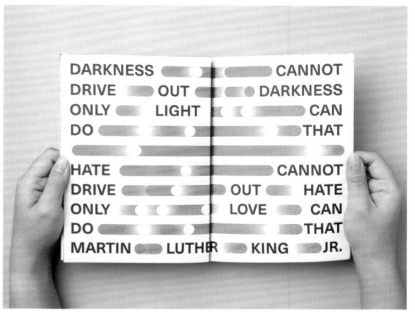

WHAT A FOLK !!!!!! 2016 • CROWD - LU • LIVE
Presents **TEAM EAR**

 PANTONE 2935 U + PANTONE 102 U

Crowd-Lu Live!

Designer: Tseng Kuo Chan
Client: TEAM EAR MUSIC

This is a visual identity design for singer Crowd Lu's concert, whose music promotes positivity and energy. The singer's character was placed in the middle of the visual, and the slogan was designed like energy beams emitted from the center. The character was printed in blue to make it more recognizable, and the secondary visuals were printed in yellow to create the bright atmosphere.

 C100 M94 Y14 K5 + C8 M30 Y100 K0

Crown of Prayers

Designer: Natalya Balnova

"The Crown of Prayers" is a silkscreen book inspired by the aesthetic of South American religious images. The book visually explores themes of death, spirituality, and salvation. The original drawings are done in black ink only, but the designer Natalya Balnova added extra colours digitally in order to bring emotional and conceptual accent.

"In most of my personal work, I approach creating images and content in a stream of consciousness or surreal manner," says Natalya. The mysterious nature of the book allows room for the individual reader to discover their own meaning, like finding their own interpretation in a dream.

 Risograph Ink: Blue + Orange

 Risograph Ink: Orange + Flat Gold

Collectors

Design Studio: Ediciones El Fuerte
Creative Directors: Juan Casal, Sofia Noceti
Designers: Juan Casal, Sofia Noceti

Ediciones El Fuerte is a small publisher project
from Buenos Aires, Argentina, that makes
zines and posters using Risograph and etching.
Coleccionistas, which means collectors, is a 44
pages zine illustrating stories about collectors
and their obsessions.

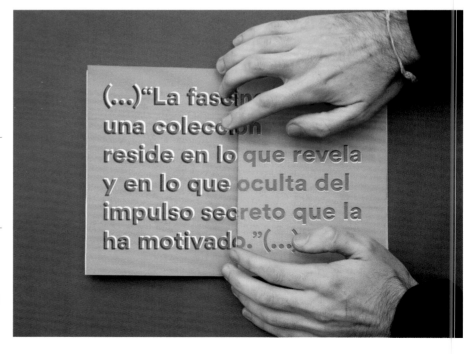

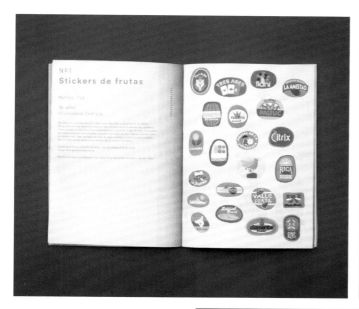

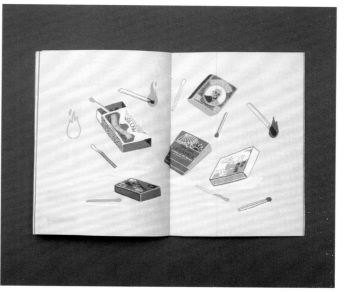

Risograph Ink:
Medium Blue+ Fluorescent Pink

Risograph Ink:
Teal + Fluorescent Orange

An Experiment in Risograph

Designers: Yu-Min Tsai, Ann-Kristin Fuchs, Heiwa Wong

A Risograph Experiment takes a deeper look at the printing technique—Risograph. Through a desktop research and studio visits, the designers present a booklet with brief introductions and guide of the technique, along with inspiring interviews with Risograph masters in Berlin and Taipei.

The main idea is to experiment the effects and possibilities of Risograph, which is known for its vibrant colours and unexpectedness. The designers take a playful approach, visualizing the characteristics through individual interpretation. As it turns out, the contrast, overlap and gradient of the colours make the booklet fun to read and worth diving into the details on every page.

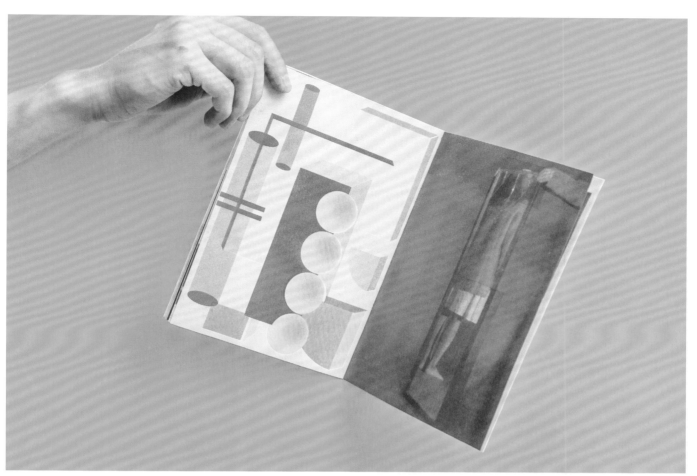

Risograph Ink: Red + Green

Christmas Cards

Design Studio: qu'est-ce que c'est design
Creative Director: Bryan Angelo Lim
Designers: Lim Jia Qing, Victoria Lee,
Deborah Neo, Liew Xin Yi

This set of Christmas cards were made by
the studio in 2015, as gifts to their clients,
partners and friends. With the iconic vibrant
red and green colours, the cards looked like
any typical Christmas cards at the first glance.
However, upon closer inspection, the receiver
would learn that there were some subtle,
hidden message within the graphics and the
text message.

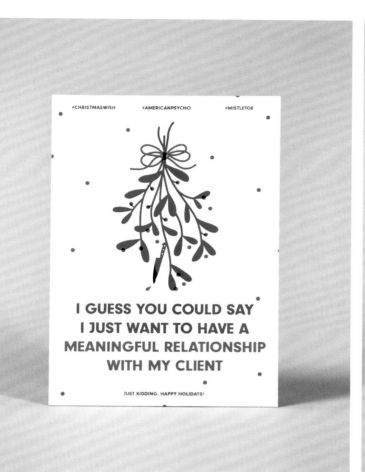

PELO N°3 — FAKE NEWS

Creative Director: Camilla Pintonato
Internal Illustrators/Writers: Alice Piaggio, Giulia Tassi, Edoardo Massa, Francesca Campagna, Elena Guglielmotti, Alice Corrain, Alessandra Belloni, Claudia Plescia, Giovanni Colaneri, Paola Momenté, Eugenio Bertozzi, Lucia Biancalana, Elisabetta D'Onghia, Giulia Piras, Virginia Gabrielli, Marco Caputo, Naida Mazzenga, Giulia Conoscenti, Giulia Pastorino, Helga Pérez Gòmez

PELO is a self-produced annual magazine founded by a collective of 21 illustrators in Italy. It's an ever-changing editorial project that bluntly addresses an irreverent subject in every issue. In the designers' opinion, the topic of each issue needs to stimulate the creators themselves, be impudent and shameless. It has to give the designers the opportunity to speak of intimate and delicate situations in an open and direct way, but without seeming trivial or exaggerated. With the Third Issue, the designers chose a very important topic for its relevance: People who nowadays read news on the Internet have never asked, but is it really true? PELO#3 will answer precisely to this question, placing the accent on some of the greatest historical and contemporary lies.

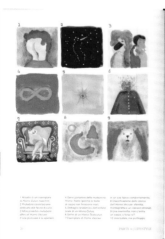

COMPRO CARAVAGGI(O) PAGO IN CONTANTI

LA CRISTOTECA

Cocco in the city

IO STO CON OLIO DI PALMA

TESTO E ILLUSTRAZIONI
LUCIA BIANCALANA

Continuano le ingiuste accuse a Olio di palma, da tempo costretto a subire ingiurie e discriminazioni di qualunque tipo.

Escluso ormai da qualsiasi tipo di relazione sociale e personale, passa le sue giornate in un luogo segreto per evitare possibili linciaggi. Olio di palma è una delle principali vittime della disinformazione contemporanea.

"Sono saturo" - così si sfoga con lo psichiatra, che lo aiuta da tempo a resistere a questa dura battaglia. "Continuano a incolpare me, invece di impegnarsi a promuovere una coltivazione più sostenibile. Non so più che fare." Se anche tu pensi che tutto questo sia un'ingiustizia, aiutaci a combattere la diffusione di questo pregiudizio: chiama il numero in sottoimpressione e lascia un messaggio a Olio di palma. Una parola di conforto può essere di aiuto alle vittime di bufale.

NUMERO VERDE: 0170 07738 135

 Risograph Ink: Teal + Fluorescent Orange

Riso Business Cards

Designer: Marine Laurent

This set of business cards is a manifestation of designer Marine Laurent's graphic universe. It consists of four types of cards, with four illustrations.

The cards were printed in Risograph. The superposition and the games of transparency make it possible to obtain new coloured shades, and also allows for printing in spot colours. The colours are brighter and it is even possible to use fluorescent colours, like the fluorescent orange used in this project.

 PANTONE 3258 C + PANTONE 219 C

Aero Jazz 2016/2017

Design Studio: Les produits de l'épicerie
Creative Director: Jérôme Grimbert
Designer: Jérôme Grimbert
Client: L'aéronef / Lille, France

For the jazz season of "L'aéronef" (concert hall in Lille, France), Les produits de l'épicerie imagined a series of eight posters, each featuring a different artist. They followed the same design concept, but changed the picture of the artist, the colour of his/her name and the date of the concert. These posters could be assembled to create one large poster/program of the season. The choice of two colours was used to create a set that looked identical to each poster. The third colour was created with the overprint.

R91 G247 B59 + R255 G51 B102

R255 G51 B102 + R17 G169 B255

R17 G169 B255 + R91 G247 B59

Goodbye Summer

Designer: Ares Pedroli
Client: School for Artistic Industries (CSIA)

The project "Goodbye Summer" was initiated at the beginning of CSIA's (School for Artistic Industries) new academic year in 2016. It contained posters, flyers and invitation for a school exhibition that showcased the works of former students. To highlight the opening date of the exhibition, the designer used a large font to convey this key information. While the text said "Forget about summer. Let's start the school", the images kept reminding people of summer, which presented an interesting contrast with the text. In terms of colour scheme, the designers chose three bright colours and used two of them on each of the posters. If viewed in a row, the comparison of colours would become more evident.

Dimentica
l'estate
inizia
la scuola

Dimentica
l'estate
inizia
la scuola

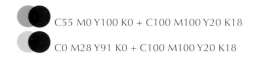

C55 M0 Y100 K0 + C100 M100 Y20 K18

C0 M28 Y91 K0 + C100 M100 Y20 K18

Sumy Extreme Style 15

Design Studio: Axen design
Creative Director: Aksion Ivankov
Designer: Aksion Ivankov
Client: Extreme Style

Sumy Extreme Style is an urban festival. In the session of 2017, the festival also added Street Art into its frame. So the designer was supposed to transmit the key message in his design, which was to combine Art and extreme.

He used two basic colours and an additional one. Deep purple was applied to the background, overpowering the meaning of Art. A bright shade of green was used in the brand graphics and represented the theme of extreme. Additional colour was orange, which was used only for advertising guests and judges of the festival in the web. The strong colour combinations resulted in a set of eye-catching graphics.

SUMY EXTREME STYLE 15

ДИВИСЬ /ДІЙ

МАНУФАКТУРА
3 / ВЕРЕСНЯ
15 / 00

#sumyextremestyle

КИРИЛО /БУРЛАКА
організатор/ведучий/чоловік
/батько та поважна людина

SUMY EXTREME STYLE 15

ДИВИСЬ /ДІЙ

МАНУФАКТУРА
3 / ВЕРЕСНЯ
15 / 00

#sumyextremestyle

ГУРТ

ЦЬОГО /РАЗУ

SUMY EXTREME STYLE 15

МАНУФАКТУРА
3 / ВЕРЕСНЯ
15 / 00

FIXED GEAR /RACES

ЦЬОГО /РАЗУ

SUMY EXTREME STYLE 15

МАНУФАКТУРА
3 / ВЕРЕСНЯ
15 / 00

/BMX

ЦЬОГО /РАЗУ

SUMY EXTREME STYLE 15

ДИВИСЬ /ДІЙ

МАНУФАКТУРА
3 / ВЕРЕСНЯ
15 / 00

#sumyextremestyle

bboy Toolskit
СУДДЯ З BREAKING

ЦЬОГО /РАЗУ

SUMY EXTREME STYLE 15

МАНУФАКТУРА
3 / ВЕРЕСНЯ
15 / 00

ЦЬОГО /РАЗУ

ZETT
/HIP-HOP/BREAKING DJ

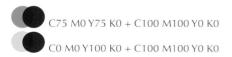

C75 M0 Y75 K0 + C100 M100 Y0 K0

C0 M0 Y100 K0 + C100 M100 Y0 K0

NYC X CATSKILLS: HEALTHY MAP

Designer: Thitipol Chaimattayompol
Client: Center for Agricultural Development & Entrepreneurship (CADE)

NYC x CATSKILLS was a project that Pratt students MS packaging design collaborated with CADE (Center for Agricultural Development & Entrepreneurship) to design a promotional material to promote local ingredients, such as egg, milk, and maple syrup from Catskills. The designer created a double-sided folding map that can be easily distributed to restaurants around New York City. The map contains the information and locations of the restaurants, cafes, and markets in Manhattan that use the organic ingredients from Catskills. On the other side displays a map of Catskills that show the location of the farms.

Since the map was distributed to urban area like Manhattan, the design has to be recognizable and stand-out among other maps and brochures. The designer was inspired by the brightness of Risograph colours, so he decided to incorporate almost pure colour tone of primary colours in his design as a representation of organic and urban look. Moreover, using two colours with newsprint paper helps emphasize the simplicity of the design. With fewer colours, but create more contrast and strong visual communication.

CATSKILLS

NORTHERN

OTSEGO

SCHOHARIA

MIDDLE

DELAWARE

GREENE

ULSTER

SOUTHERN

SULLIVAN

OTSEGO COUNTY*
SCHOHARIA COUNTY*
ONEONTA
COOPERTOWN
COBLESKILL
GREENVILE
WORCESTER

DELAWARE COUNTY*
GREENE COUNTY*
DELHI
STAMFORD
WINDHAM
WALTON
HUNTER
GREENVILLE

SULLIVAN COUNTY*
ULSTER COUNTY*
LIVINGSTON MANOR
LIBERTY
MONTICELLO
KINGSTON
WOODSTOCK
ULSTER
PINE HILL

LIVE LONGER LIVE HEALTHIER

SAY GOODBYE TO:
SYNTHETIC PESTICIDES
CHEMICAL FERTILIZERS
IRRADIATION
INDUSTRIAL SOLVENTS
CHEMICAL FOOD ADDITIVES

NYC LIFE   CATSKILLS

One study showed that organic fruits and veggies contain 27% more vitamin C, 21.1% more iron, 29.3% more magnesium, 13.6% more phosphorus, and 18% more polyphenols. The only US beef that has been free of the fatal prion brain disease Creutzfeldt-Jakob, is organic.

Researchers have found that there is an average of 600% more salicylic acid in organic soups, and that organic carrot and coriander soup contains 1,040 nanograms of it, compared with only 20 nanograms in typical nonorganic soups.

The fruits, vegetables daily products you buy at the farmers market are the freshest and tastiest available. The products brought directly to you no long-distance shopping, no gassing to simulate the ripening process, no sitting for weeks in storage. This food is as real as it gets fresh from the farm.

Family farmers need your support, now that large agribusiness dominates food production in the U.S. Small family farms have a hard time competing in the food marketplace.

DAILY PRODUCTS (d)

Bovine Valley Farm (607) 746-8192
77 Huff Rd, Delhi, NY

Burn Ayr Farm (607) 746-7287
21031 NY-28, Delhi, NY

ByeBrook Farms (607) 538-9706
Co Rd 18, Bloomville, NY

Dirty Girl Farm (845) 676-4000
539 Perch Lake Rd, Andes, NY

Eagle Hollow Farm (607) 865-7215
2004 Mac Gibbon Hollow Rd,
Walton, NY

East Brook Farm (607) 746-9142
2253 County Highway 22, Walton, NY

Getnamore Farm (607) 832-4472
2363 Bramley Mountain Road,
Bovina Center, NY

Gray Goose Farm (607) 746-3645
83 Maggie Hoag Road
Delancey, NY

Crystal Valley Farms (845) 254-4005
253 County Route 3
Halcott Center, NY

Dirai's Dairy Farm (845) 4824301
1345 Shandelee Road, Livingston
Manor, NY

VEGGIES & MEAT (e)

Applegarth Farms (607) 638-5784
137 Axtell Road, Maryland, NY

Eternal Flame Farm (607) 865-7597
61 Conclin road, Walton, NY

Rich Farm (607) 538-1317
13075 County Highway 18, Hobart, NY

Story Farms LLC (518) 678-5761
4640 State Route 32, Catskill, NY

Fall Brook Farm (607) 326-2892
2590 West Settlement Road,
Roxbury, NY

HONEY & MAPLE (f)

Berry Brook Farm (607) 267-0194
2369 Back River Road, Delancy, NY

SaJoBe Farms (607) 865-4402
286 Hoyt Road, Walton, NY

Horton Hill Farm (607) 652-9450
127 Horton Road, Jefferson, NY

Nectar Hills Farm (518) 678-5758
393 Peelor Road, Schenevus, NY

Buck Hill Farm (607) 652-7040
185 Fuller Road, Jefferson, NY

Good Fields (607) 859-2227
1277 Copes Corner Road, South
New Berlin, NY

Tree Juice (607) 267-0194
251 Rider Hollow Road Arkville, NY

Catskill Provision (518) 947-0244
244 Delaware Lake Road, Long

MT Acrec Farm (607) 267-0141
1933 MacDougall Road, Oneonta, NY

Pure Mountain Honey (607) 865-1718
Walton, NY

Catskill Provision (845) 418-1432
244 Delaware Lake Road
Long Eddy, NY

RSK Farm (518) 299-3129
13255 State Route 23A, Prattsville, NY

Cold Spring Farm (518) 254-4268
4953 State Route 145, Lawyersville, NY

Heirloom Acres (845) 856-1722
23 Main St. Narrowsburg, NY

Edge Wood (845) 245-9874
22 Lasher Road, Big India, NY

Keider's Farm (845) 626-1131
5755 Route 209, Kerhonkson, NY

Griffin Conners (315-242-7401
189-829 Brush Ridge Road
Fleischmann, NY

CADE

MANHATTAN, NY

HEY NEW YORKER
SAY HI TO:
CATSKILLS
LOCAL FARMERS
TRUE NUTRIENTS
FRESHNESS

NYC EATERS NYC HEALTHIER

ORGANIC FOOD   LOCAL FARMS

DOWN TOWN

MID TOWN

UP TOWN

CENTRAL PARK

SOHO
NOHO
BOWERY
NOLITA
LITTLE ITALY
EAST VILLAGE
WEST VILLAGE
LOWER EAST SIDE
GREENWICH VILAGE

KIPS BAY
CHELSEA
TIMES SQUARE
HUDSON YARDS
UNION SQUARE
HUDSON YARDS
HELL'S KITCHEN
MADISON SQUARE
STUYVESANT SQUARE

HARLEM
YORKVILLE
MARBLE HILL
FORT GEORGE
UPPER WEST SIDE
UPPER MANHATTAN
WASHINGTON HEIGHTS

One study showed that organic fruits and veggies daily products you buy at the farmers market are the freshest and tastiest available. The products brought directly to you no long-distance shopping, no gassing to simulate the ripening process, no sitting for weeks in storage. This food is as real as it gets fresh from the farm.

One study showed that organic fruits and veggies daily products you buy at the farmers market are the freshest and tastiest available. The products brought directly to you no long-distance shopping, no gassing to simulate the ripening process, no sitting for weeks in storage. This food is as real as it gets fresh from the farm.

Researchers have found that there is an average of 600% more salicylic acid in organic soups, and that organic carrot and coriander soup contains 1,040 nanograms of it, compared with only 20 nanograms in typical nonorganic soups.

Family farmers need your support, now that large agribusiness dominates food production in the U.S. Small family farms have a hard time competing in the food marketplace.

RESTAURANTS (a)

a1 Hu Kitchen
78 5th Ave (at E 14th St), New
York, NY

a2 Bareburger
153 8th Ave (btwn 17th & 18th
St), New York, NY

a3 Siggy's Good Food
292 Elizabeth St (btwn E Houston
& Bleecker St), New York, NY

a4 ABC Kitchen
35 E 18th St (btwn Broadway &
Park Ave S), New York, NY

a5 The Fat Radish
17 Orchard St, New York, NY

a6 Bubby's
120 Hudson St (btwn Franklin &
Moore St), New York, NY

a7 Candle 79.0
154 E 79th St (at Lexington Ave)
New York, NY

a8 Foragers Table.9
300 W 22nd St (at 8th Ave), New
York, NY

a9 Blue Hill
75 Washington Place
New York, NY

MARKETS (b)

b1 Union Square Greenmarket
1 Union Sq W, New York, NY

b2 Bubby's
120 Hudson St (btwn Franklin &
Moore St), New York, NY

b3 Fairway Market9.0
2328 12th Ave, New York, NY

b4 A Matter of Health, Inc
1347 First Ave, New York, NY

b5 Lifethyme
410 Ave Of The Americas
New York, NY

b6 Ali Baba Organic Marketplace
1 Mott St, New York, NY

b7 Commodities Natural Market
165 1st Ave New York, NY

b8 Essex St Market
911 8th Avenue New York, NY

b9 Fairway Market
550 2nd Ave New York, NY

b10 A Matter of Health, Inc
1347 First Ave, New York, NY

b11 Inwood Greenmarket
Isham St & Seaman Ave
New York, NY

CAFES (c)

c1 Union Square Greenmarket
1 Union Sq W, New York, NY

c2 Westerly Natural Market
911 8th Avenue, New York, NY

c3 Fairway Market9.0
2328 12th Ave, New York, NY

c4 A Matter of Health, Inc
1347 First Ave New York, NY

c5 Lifethyme
410 Ave Of The Americas
New York, NY

c6 Ali Baba Organic Marketplace
1 Mott St, New York, NY

c7 Commodities Natural Market
165 1st Ave, New York, NY

c8 Essex St Market
120 Essex St. New York, NY

c9 Fairway Market
550 2nd Ave, New York, NY

c10 A Matter of Health, Inc
1347 First Ave, New York, NY

c11 Inwood Greenmarket
Isham St & Seaman Ave
New York, NY

CADE

PANTONE Green U + PANTONE Violet U

PANTONE 342 U + PANTONE 471 U

Théâtre Dunois
2016/2017 & 2017/2018

Design Studio: Les produits de l'épicerie
Creative Director: Marieke Offroy
Designer: Marieke Offroy
Client: Théâtre Dunois / Paris, France

Les produits de l'épicerie has been working since 2014 for the Théâtre Dunois in Paris, which is a theatre targeting young audiences.

The designer Marieke Offroy proposed to create illustrations from hybrid animals, and for the latest season (17/18), she has imagined and drawn "strange beings", a kind of mutation between human and animal parts. Since 2014, the studio has been working with two colours for the communication design of Théâtre Dunois, which has made it possible to strengthen the visual identity of the theatre, and maintain printing economy.

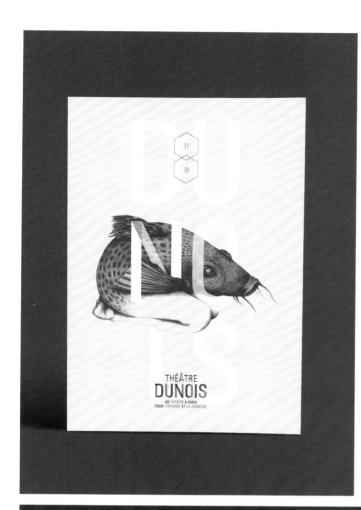

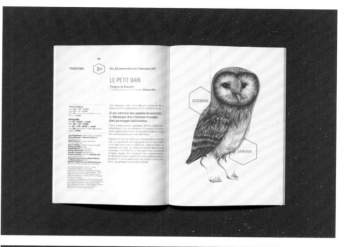

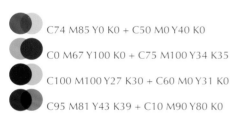

C74 M85 Y0 K0 + C50 M0 Y40 K0

C0 M67 Y100 K0 + C75 M100 Y34 K35

C100 M100 Y27 K30 + C60 M0 Y31 K0

C95 M81 Y43 K39 + C10 M90 Y80 K0

Kandinsky Typeface

Design Studio: K95
Creative Director: Danilo De Marco
Designer: Danilo De Marco

Kandisky typeface is a set of experimental font inspired by Russian artist Wassily Kandisky and his book "Point and Line to Plane". Every lowercase letter has a set of lines, while the uppercase has points and lines. To advertise Kandisky typeface, K95 designed several posters using duotone technique, where the image fits perfectly with the letters' shapes. One of these posters included a photo of the artist intersected with his own name.

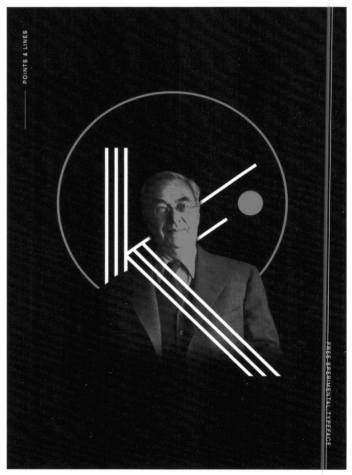

KANDINSKY

FREE SPERIMENTAL TYPEFACE

PANTONE 359 C + PANTONE 2593 C

Graphic Design Brochure

Designers: Isabel Beltrán, Pamela Sada
Client: University of Monterrey

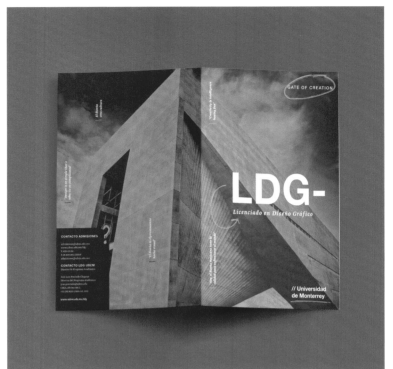

This editorial project's purpose was to create a new booklet for the bachelor in graphic design at the University of Monterrey, laying out in a creative way all the available classes, information about campus and the different facilities, school exchanges, and award-winning student projects, for new alumni to learn about in an easy and dynamic way.

The concept is inspired by the brain and its different hemispheres: the logical and the creative. Both are crucial for its proper functioning, and both are necessary characteristics for design students. The right hemisphere, the creative, is represented with handmade organic details, and the left side, the rational, is represented with grids and modular details. As for the use of colours, green is associated with finances and ambition, while purple is linked with creativity, which combined together make up a powerful duo.

PANTONE 199 + PANTONE 2736

PANTONE 199 + PANTONE 803

Asian Diva:
the Muse and the Monster

Design Studio: studio fnt
Designer: Jaemin Lee
Curators: Regina Shin, Yongwoo Lee
Client: Seoul Museum of Art

This was an identity design project for an exhibition, Asian Diva: the Muse and the Monster, which was held in Seoul Museum of Art. It includes posters, catalogs, exhibition graphics and other printed matters. This exhibition introduced contemporary art together with the icons of Korean pop music in 60s and 70s as a prism that embodies the experiences of the post-colonial era that penetrate Asia, from the lives and voices of women, issues of gender and sexuality to Cold War and dictatorship.

For this project, studio fnt made a Korean retro style logotype and utilized complementary colours to symbolize the dramatic era. The woman in the two posters is Kim Chooja, who was one of the most well-known divas in 70s in Korea. The combination of iconic woman, perspective letters and primary colours express the energy of oppressed ones in an absurd period of time.

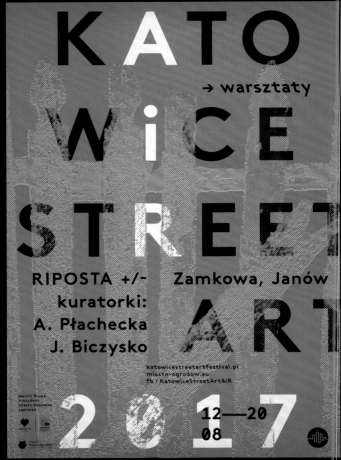

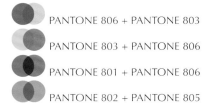

PANTONE 806 + PANTONE 803

PANTONE 803 + PANTONE 806

PANTONE 801 + PANTONE 806

PANTONE 802 + PANTONE 805

Katowice Street Art AiR 2017

Designer: Marta Gawin
Client: Instytucja Kultury Katowice – Miasto Ogrodów

In 2017, Katowice Street Art Festival transformed into Residential Katowice Street Art AiR program. A change of a formula required also a change of thinking, rejecting old habits and common ways of operating; it required a revolution. The invited Artists gradually familiarized themselves with the space. Each at their own pace. A number of interesting projects were created.

To visualize the process of transition not only of the festival's program but also the transition taking place in the societies, the new visual language was developed. Broken walls were chosen as graphic representation of the need of emancipation. Barbed wires referred also to the actual political situation.

Gradation

$1+1=\infty$

PANTONE 2563 C +PANTONE 2726 C

Macau Booth of "Hong Kong Book Fair 2017"

Design Studio: SomethingMoon Design
Designer: Chiwai Cheang
Client: Macau Foundation

This project reflects the designer's contemplation about literature. Here is the designer's own word of his design idea: "I compare literature to light and show, as we are both inside it and outside of it. I expand the canvas to the outside of the common customs, but also narrow it down to the place where a glimmer could shine through the crack in the book."

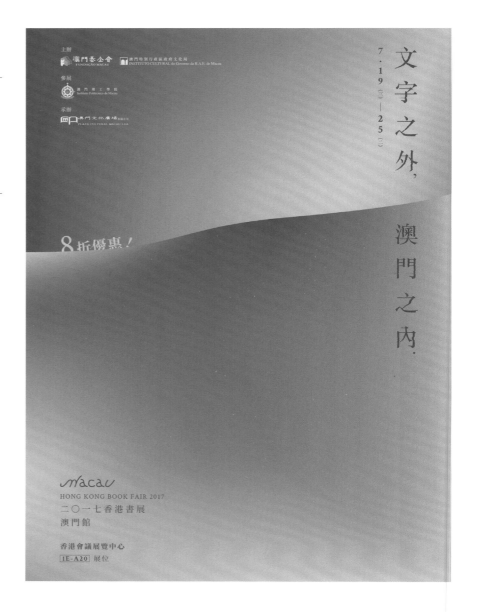

 PANTONE 1555 U +
PANTONE Reflex Blue U

Espacios Mutualistas

Design Studio: Estudio Machete
Designers: Laura Cárdenas, Laura Daza
Photographer: Sebastián Cruz Roldán
Client: Artistic project Espacios Mutualistas

Espacios Mutualistas (Mutualist Spaces) is a
project that recreates forgotten and non-existent
community, historic places in Bogotá city,
Colombia, through artistic interventions.
It consists of the creation of 24 different covers
applying the duotone technique. These pieces
recreated a variety of fictional places with multiple
formal features and emphasized the structural
singularity of each space. As a result, the process
of creating non-existent locations produced new
unreal extensions.

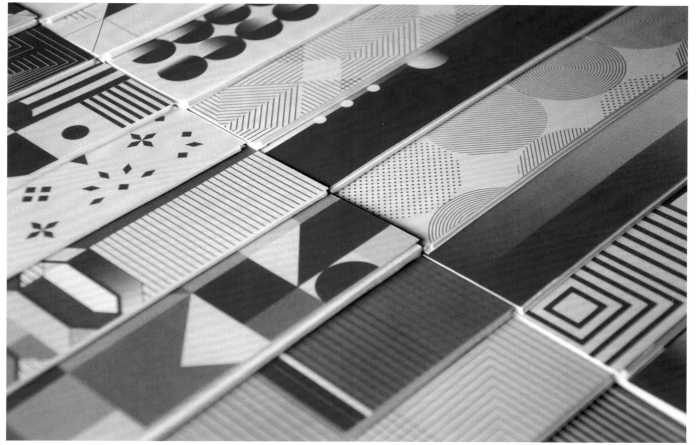

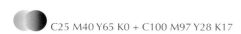

C25 M40 Y65 K0 + C100 M97 Y28 K17

Art Summit Indonesia

Creative Director: Ritter Willy Putra
Designers: Hendri Siman Santosa, Utari Kennedy, Edwin
Client: The Ministry of Education and Culture, Republic of Indonesia

Art Summit Indonesia is an international festival initiated by Republic of Indonesia under the ministry of education and culture, beginning in 1995. Through this festival, "Indonesia invites the world", especially in the field of contemporary performing arts from music, dance, and theatre.

This rebranding project was aimed to set a benchmark for Art Summit Indonesia as the new center of art in the global sphere by repositioning Indonesia's contemporary performing art into the new perspective. The challenge of this project was to create a flexible visual identity for Art Summit Indonesia, both as an organization and also a triennale festival.

Two geometrical shapes combined with different colour treatment – solid and gradient – are intended to create a contemporary look and presenting the sense of movement to the identity.

 PANTONE 7736 U + PANTONE 7604 U

PANTONE 296 U + PANTONE 7507 U

Gabriel Tan Studio

Design Studio: Roots
Creative Director: Jonathan Yuen
Designers: Jonathan Yuen, Gabriel Tan
Client: Gabriel Tan Studio

Gabriel Tan Studio is the newly formed eponymous studio of Gabriel Tan, an industrial designer working between Singapore, Barcelona and New York, whose work spans across the disciplines of product, spatial and interior design.

Roots were engaged to conceptualise an identity system for the studio. They devised a colour gradient system that is simple and visually striking to represent the cross disciplinary nature. Each studio personnel in turn personalises their individual unique duotone gradient colours to be used in business cards and studio stationery. The design solution allows the identity to expand as the studio grows.

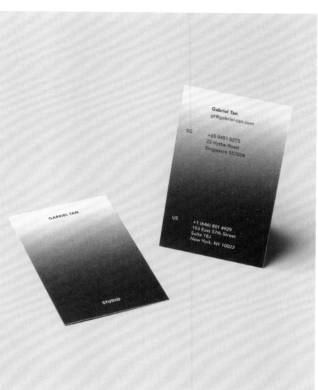

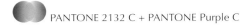 PANTONE 2132 C + PANTONE Purple C

Beaujolais Nouveau

Design Studio: Explicit Design Studio
Creative Director: Hunor Kátay
Designers: Hunor Kátay, Sebestyén Németh,
Szilárd Kovács, Márton Ács

Beaujolais is a historical province and a wine producing region in France. It is located in the north of Lyon, and covers parts of the south of the Saône-et-Loire département. The region is known internationally for its long tradition of wine-making, and more recently for the enormously popular Beaujolais nouveau. Beaujolais nouveau is a red wine made from Gamay Noir à Jus blanc grape, better known simply as Gamay. It is the most popular vin de primeur, a purple-pink wine reflecting its youth, bottled only 6-8 weeks after harvest. This pigmentation is represented by the colour scheme of the project. This stylish texture is paired with clear and contemporary graphic elements that embody the juvenility and elegance of the Beaujolais nouveau wine.

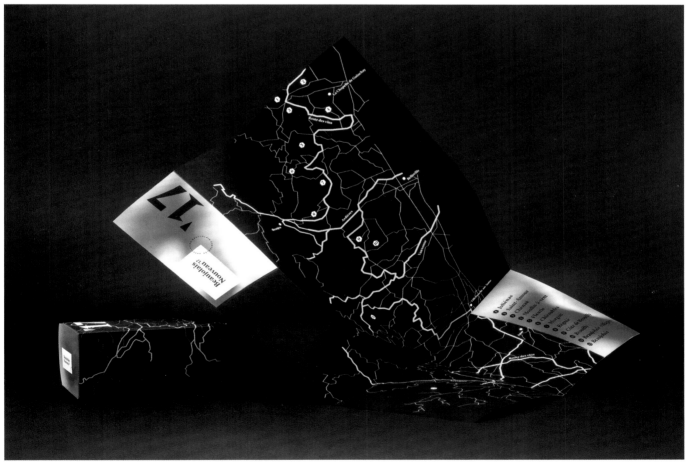

193

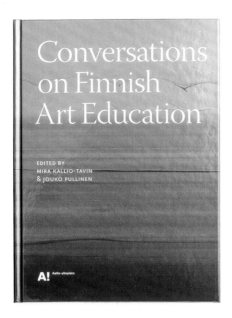

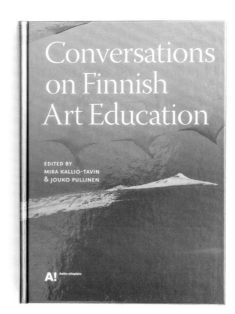

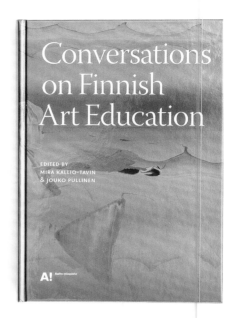

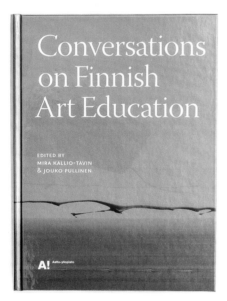

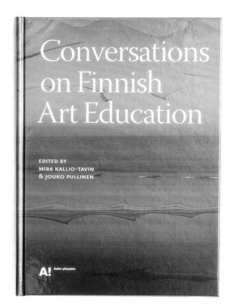

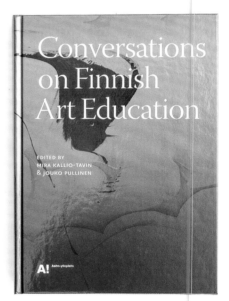

 PANTONE 294 + PANTONE 876

Conversations
on Finnish Art Education

Design Studio: Merkitys
Creative Director: Safa Hovinen
Designer: Safa Hovinen
Client: Aalto ARTS Books

This book brings together 22 articles from the field of art education to celebrate the 100th anniversary of art education in Finland. The studio decided to create a festive but dignified feel for the book. The most natural choice for colour in a Finland-themed book was blue because blue is part of the Finnish flag. Another colour chosen was the metallic copper, which is often present in Finnish architecture. These two colours create a dynamic combination with both hue and material feel.

Another important factor was to create an element of surprise. After research, Merkitys studio printed the covers in silk screen with the print operators stroking the screen to live-mix the colours together in random ways. The result is a unique series of covers: each copy is truly different as if a painter has painted them.

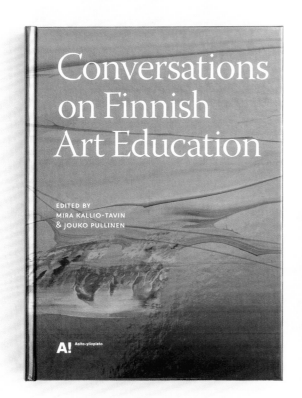

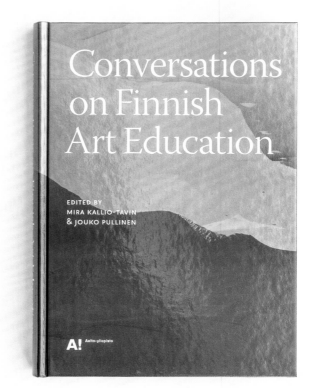

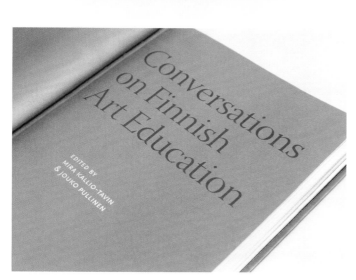

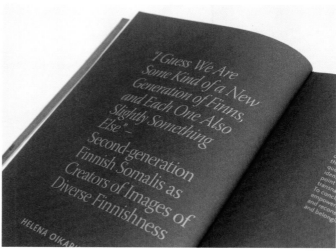

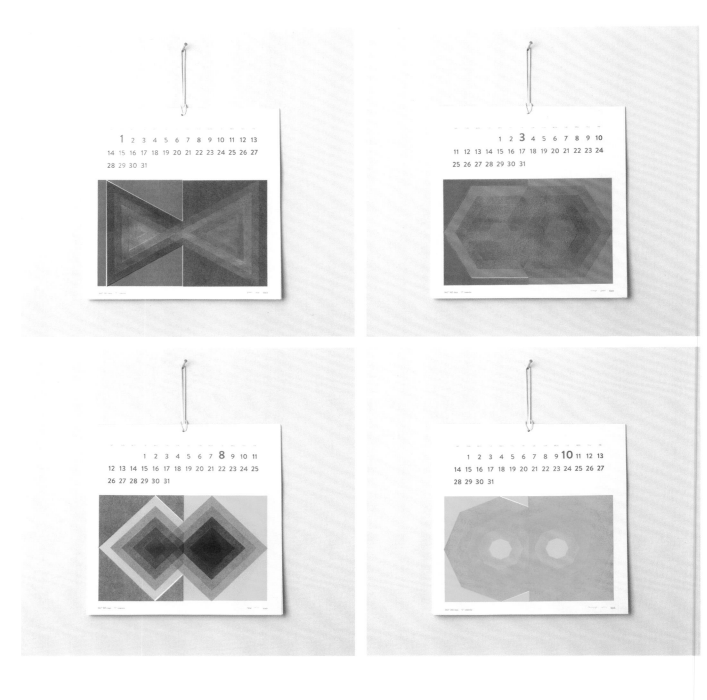

Risograph Ink: Green + Blue

Risograph Ink: Green + Orange

Risograph Ink: Blue + Yellow

Risograph Ink: Yellow + Orange

Risograph Ink: Fluorescent Orange + Lavender

Risograph Ink: Blue + Fluorescent Pink

Risograph Ink: Lavender + Yellow

Risograph Ink: Green + Fluorescent Pink

360° 365 days . 2017 Calendar

Design Studio: O.OO Risograph & Design Room / *Creative Directors:* Pip Lu, Panyuchou / *Designers:* Pip Lu, Panyuchou

The project 360° 365 days takes the shape of circle as the starting point. When connecting the points on the circumference, different polygons are created. The studio used the technique of diffusion, equidistant cutting and the crossover of two colours to create the third colour. Combining with Risograph printing, this experiment of colours rendered unexpected outcomes.

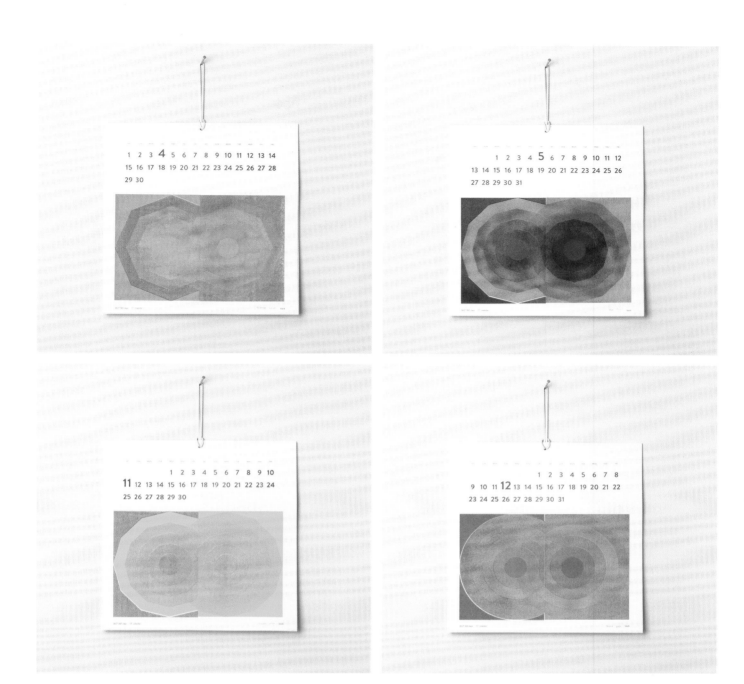

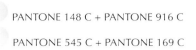

PANTONE 148 C + PANTONE 916 C

PANTONE 545 C + PANTONE 169 C

Kigive Moon Festival Gift Box

Design Studio: W/H Design Studio
Art Director: Hua Lin
Designers: Sean Lin, Pei Hsu
Project Manager: Jenny Lin
Printer: ICE Printing
Photographer: Chifan Chung

This project used soft-tone gradient to represent the liquid state of the tea water and the different intensity of fragrance. Light green and chestnut colour stand for Eastern tea, plain and rustic; while pink and blue show the romantic flavour of Western tea.

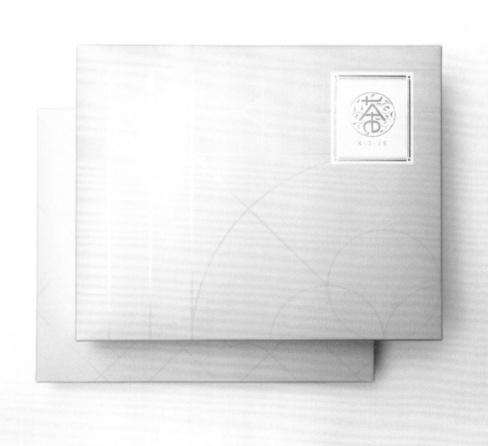

 PANTONE 2736 C + PANTONE 805 C

GET THE NEW ART! – HUFA Open Day 2017

Designer: Marcell Kazsik
Client: Hungarian University of Fine Arts (HUFA)

This project is the open day design for the Hungarian University of Fine Arts. This institution is Hungary's most influential university specialized in art and it aims for educating individual artists of a European level. The goal of this event was to propagate contemporary art.

For the visual appearance, designer Marcell Kazsik used two pale colours as a smooth background and mixed them with a massive type, named Druk wide by "Commercial Type" Type foundry. The design idea came from the impression of the rising sun. For the printing of the posters, he used a traditional screen printing technique, but opted for offset printing for the brochures, digital printing for the stickers and other materials.

Lina Gutiérrez – Estrategia Digita

Creative and Art Director: Lully Duque
Designer: Lully Duque
Photographer: Luis Carlos Díaz
Client: Lina Gutiérrez

Lina Gutiérrez – Estrategia Digital is a brand founded by a Colombian communicator that is focused on providing advice on digital strategies to multiple multinational companies.

What differentiates Lina Gutierrez from her competitors is simply put, "common sense". Most of their successful cases are based on simple, well-executed solutions that bring good results. Therefore, for the development of this brand, a decision was made to create a sufficiently open system that demonstrates the versatility and dynamism of the brand through very simple elements.

All these elements, which are mixed and combined, make the receiver appreciate a dynamic and constantly changing brand, but that keeps a graphic unity in all its presentations. Despite the multiple combinations that can be generated in the use of this brand, it should always be clear that it is the same system of identity. The colour palette gives this brand contemporary and versatile feelings, and reflects the dynamics of the digital world through the use of solid tones and gradients.

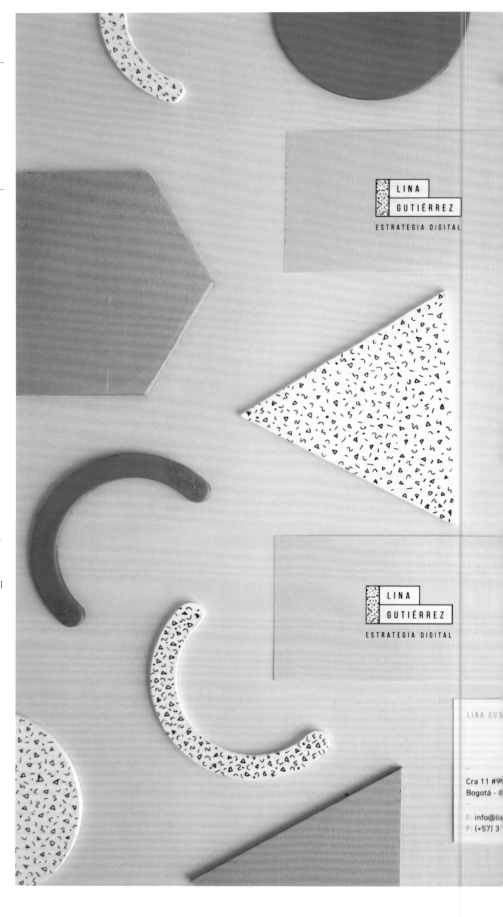

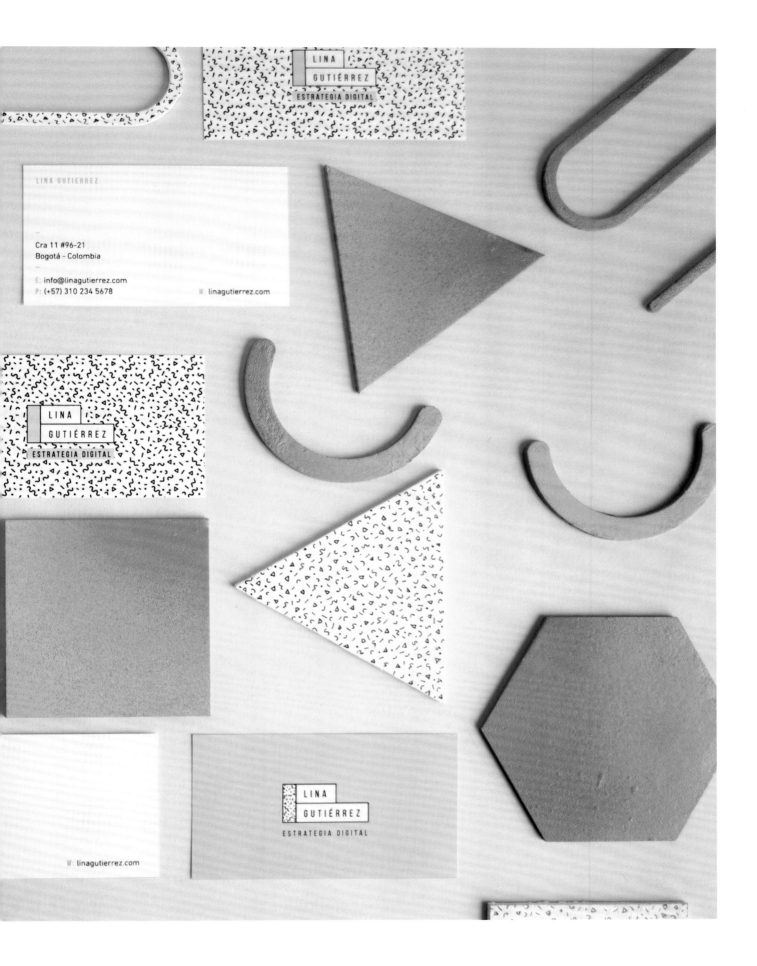

 C0 M90 Y40 K0 + C85 M0 Y40 K0

Museum of Modern Typography

Designers: Beatrice Bianchet, Gloria Maggioli

This is the identity for the fictional museum of modern typography. The designers raised an interesting questions: what is typography today? The reality of modern letters is the conjunction of different practices: calligraphy, illustration, digital foundries, visual layout. These colours were chosen to connect the historical issue of typography in a contemporary context in which letters became something of malleable and personal.

R60 G199 B210 + R255 G245 B63

Fashion Ambient –
Fashion Talk Show
#Series 04

Designer: Youvi. Chow
Client: Cultural Power Institute

Two Fashion Talk Shows are held every year at the Mix-Place in Shanghai, China. The theme of 2017AW is Fashion Ambient, literally conveying the feeling of one's being surrounded by cheerful and innovative atmosphere of fashion. Therefore, the designer was thinking of something young but not frivolous; dynamic yet deeply intense; gradient however sharp; and curving nevertheless floating, in order to make this atmosphere sensationally abstract. She feels that it would be more creative when the work is being appreciated abstractly: Abstraction urges imagination to run wild. These blissful yet contradicting elements not only merge but influence each other to create newness which people can touch and feel, rather than just seeing on the screen. The neon blue is mixed up with the yellow gradients so brightly and contrasting enough to draw attention.

FASHION TALKSHOW
时尚谈话录

Series 4

FASHION AMBIENT

策划

文化 艺术

呈现

THE MIX-PLACE
衡山·和集

支持
上海时装周
SHANGHAI FASHION WEEK

YMOYNOT

YNOT SHOW ROOM

/ 10.13 (FRI) /

19:30-21:00
The beautiful unknown 美丽的未知
Gene Krell_VOGUE/GQ亚洲区创意总监

/ 10.14 (SAT) /

14:30-16:00
《VISION》杂志 视觉设计的无序之序
孙 初_艺术总监

17:00-18:30
NOWNESS时尚短片创造力
叶晓薇_现代传播集团时尚编辑总监
肖耀辉_NOWNESS中文网主编

19:00-20:30
设计师现场
dido_deepmoss设计师
郭 晓_视觉设计师

/ 10.15 (SUN) /

14:30-16:00
时装与文化考古
徐小喵_时尚撰稿人

16:30-18:00
设计师现场
Angus Chiang_入围LVMH大奖的华裔设计师

19:00-20:30
你对时尚界最大的10个误解
林 剑_时尚评论人

上海市衡山路880号
衡山·和集 Dr.White

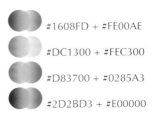 #1608FD + #FE00AE

#DC1300 + #FEC300

#D83700 + #0285A3

#2D2BD3 + #E00000

Super Gradient

Designer: Song Ho Jong

This series of posters are designer Song Ho Jong's daily practice of designing gradient posters. He doesn't use pictures and source images, but fully relies on his creativity and new ideas, which he think is a great way to accumulate experiences and strengthen his skills.

SUPER
GRADIENT
#22

One Day One Poster

Gradient
Psycho

SONG HOJONG 2017 – 2018

SONG HOJONG 2017 – 2018

One Day
One Poster

@Song Hojong

2017. 03. 30

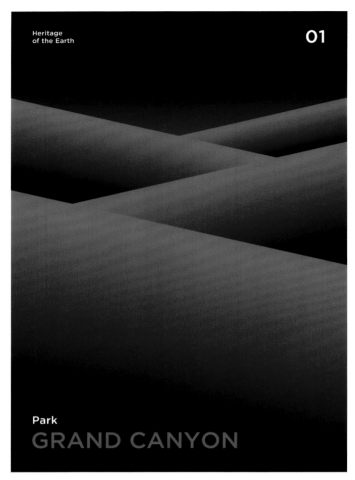

Park

GRAND CANYON

Trench

MARIANA

Mountain Ranges

HIMALAYAS

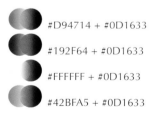

#D94714 + #0D1633

#192F64 + #0D1633

#FFFFFF + #0D1633

#42BFA5 + #0D1633

Heritage of the Earth

Designer: Song Ho Jong

In this project, the designer wanted to raise people's awareness of protecting nature. Some well-known natural sights, like the Himalayas and Mariana trench, are beautifully presented using gradient technique. In designer Song Ho Jong's own word, "Nature protection is easy and simple. My design is also easy and simple."

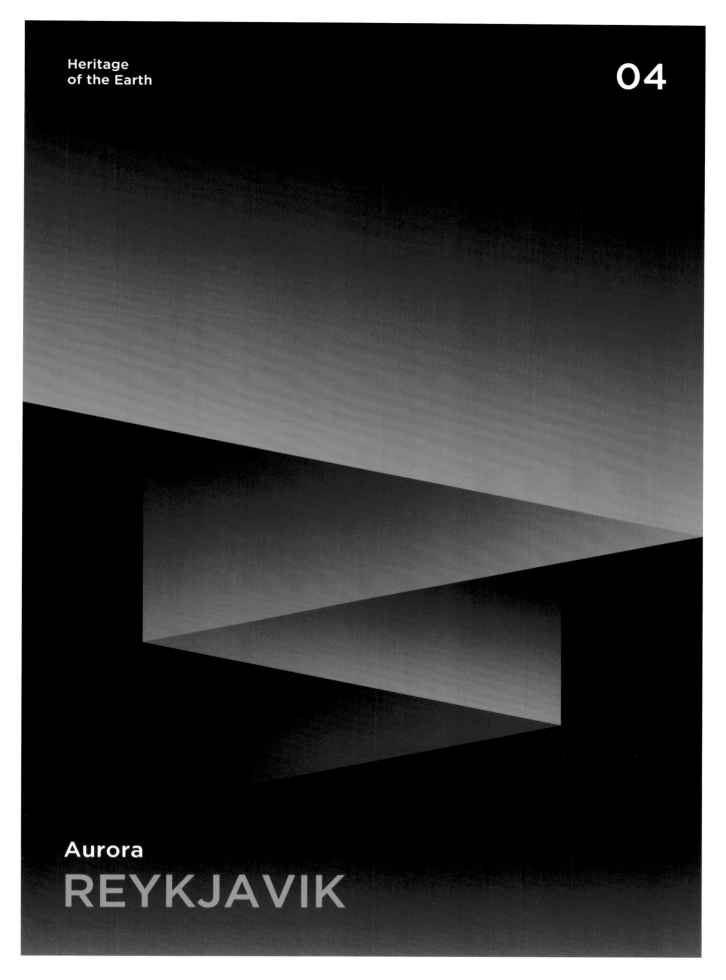

Aurora
REYKJAVIK

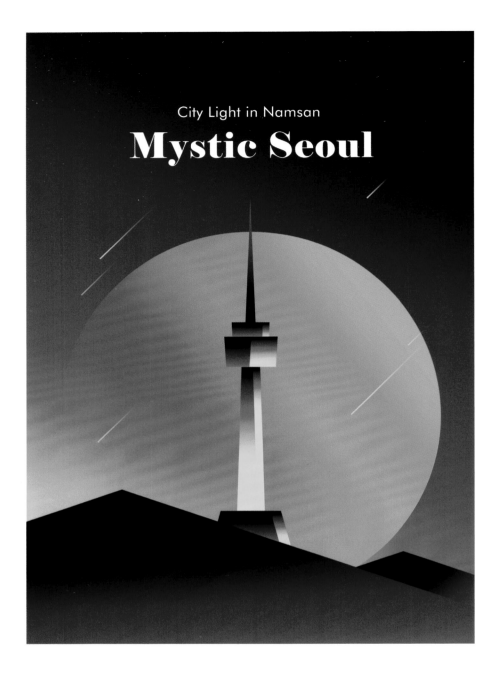

City Light in Namsan

Mystic Seoul

#FC3E00 + #1ED2C7

#070DDF + #DD0F36

#F66202 + #0049A8

Mystic Seoul

Designer: Song Ho Jong

With these dreamy gradient posters, the designer invited readers to explore the night scene of Seoul. He took a bold approach to using colours and created strong contrast, which depicted the liveliness and charm of the Seoul city.

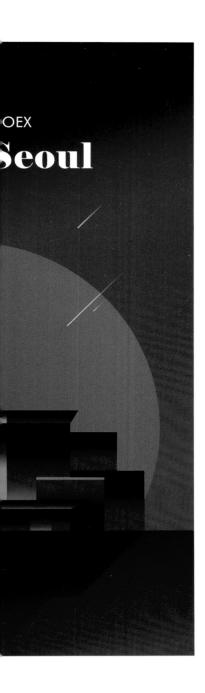

OEX

Seoul

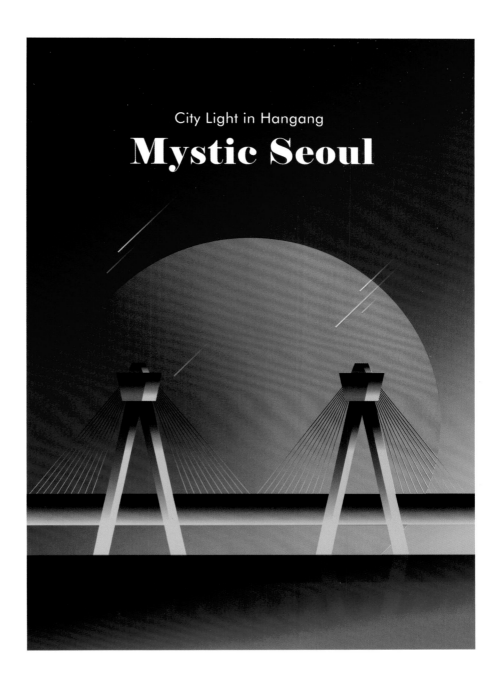

City Light in Hangang

Mystic Seoul

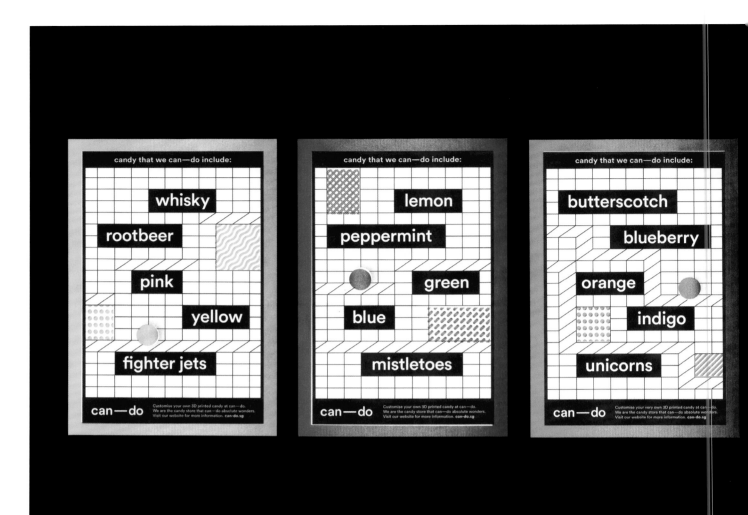

Risograph Ink: Yellow + Fluorescent Pink

Risograph Ink: Green + Blue

Risograph Ink: Orange + Purple

Can – do Confectionery

Designer: Adelia Lim

Can – do is a branding project for a 3D candy printing confectionery. Can – do's 3D candy printing is a refreshing take on sugar confectionery, allowing for the customization of form, flavor and colour effortlessly. With a playful and bold personality, the brand targets adventurous risk takers who are unafraid to try new things. While the primary logo is mainly used on corporate stationery, the secondary logo adopts a flexible identity, where the "can" and "do" are always placed at different positions on a 3D-grid. The duo-tagline, "candy that can – do wonders" and "candy with a can – do attitude", are used in various promotional materials and emphasizes further on the idea of endless candy possibilities. The project covers a wide range of touchpoints from posters to packaging. Vibrantly clad in duo-tone Risograph colours, the designs reflect and represent the eye-catching, multicoloured attributes of the product itself.

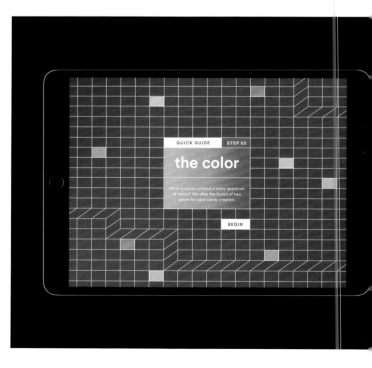

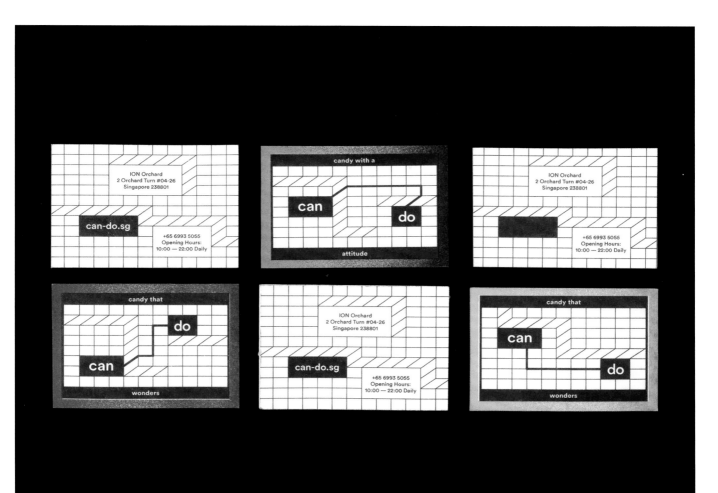

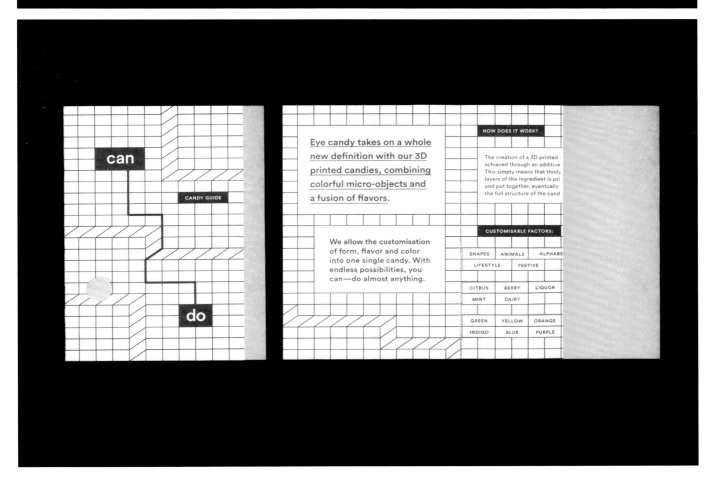

 R0 G155 B167 + R220 G31 B87

Open HCI 2016

Design Studio: OpenHCI'16 Committee
Creative Director: Chieh-Ting Lee
Designers: Chieh-Ting Lee, Jar Chen
Clients: NTUST, NTU, NCCU

Open HCI is an annual student-organized workshop that lasts for five days, where students from both design and technology background are recruited and work as teams. The workshop focuses on pursuing radical and exciting ideas instead of conservative projects, and the topic of 2016 is "GITOPIA", which stands for a balanced, futuristic and harmonious future world. After five days of brainstorming, discussion and prototyping, in the final demonstration, all the teams bring great proposals such as intelligent products, interactive programs, images and films, in both the form of slide presentation and live demo.

Designer Chieh-Ting Lee designed the identity and website for this event, following two principles. First, two colours, red and blue, stand for humans and technology respectively; second, the movement of these two colours reflects the relationship between humans and technology. Accordingly, there are different types of visual image instead of a static one for the identified system.

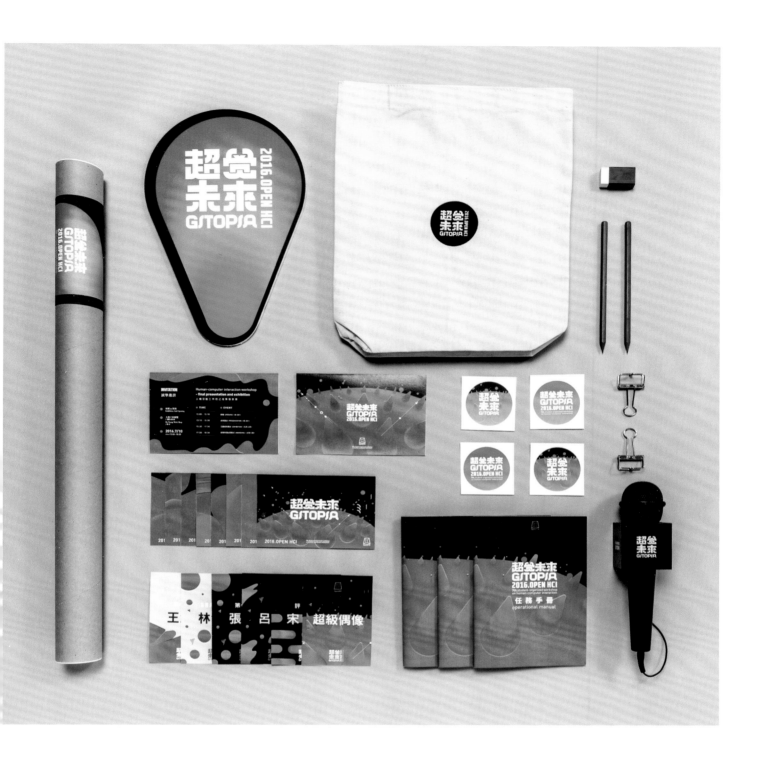

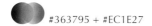 #363795 + #EC1E27

Last Wave

Creative Directors: Whitney Bolin, Axel Vagnard
Designers: Whitney Bolin, Axel Vagnard

Last Wave is an alternative music festival that could rock the Grand Palais in Paris, France. As a last hoorah to celebrate the end of summer, it would be one last show, one last time to get together with friends, one last wave of fun before going back to school and work.

Sharp and thin, the white title in Brandon Grotesque contrasts sharply while balancing with the rich, vibrant background. Inspired by the beauty of nature, the concept design's two inverted gradients symbolize a single rising, rolling crest encircling the last sunset of summer. The warmth of the fading sunlight radiates through a rich vermillion red, ebbing into the cool ultramarine blue of the deep waters.

This bold yet elegant colour scheme is implemented throughout the event's visual communication including posters, a program booklet, tickets, postcards, and invitations.

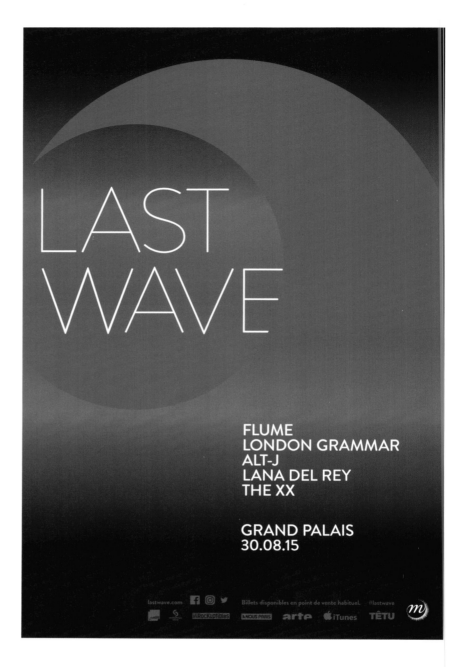

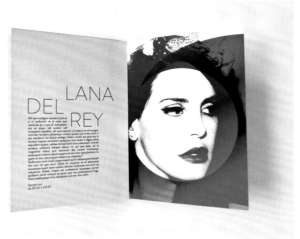

PANTONE 199 C + PANTONE 5265 C
PANTONE 172 C + PANTONE 7684 C

Artloop Festival 2016

Design Studio: Uniforma
Creative Director: Michał Mierzwa
Designer: Michał Mierzwa
Client: Artloop Festival

The key word of the 5th edition of the Artloop Festival was "cumulation". The main theme refers to the concept of a cosmic black hole, the cumulation of particles and their eventual visual forms when they're under the force of single energy bringing them together.

Within the scope of the festival, a number of elements were designed, including official poster, placards, printed promotional materials, and a TV spot.

Colour palette refers to the main idea of the design concept. Colours of energy, high temperature combined with colours that remind black hole and space.

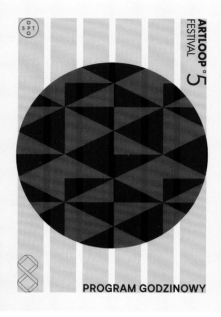

 ARTLOOP °5
FESTIVAL

ARTLOOP °5
FESTIVAL

PROGRAM GODZINOWY

ARTLOOP Festival otwiera miasto na sztukę i sztukę na miasto, scalając/loopując wybrane przestrzenie w centrum Sopotu licznymi działaniami/akcjami z zakresu sztuk wizualnych w powiązaniu z innymi sztukami. **ARTLOOP** otwiera się na dynamiczną interakcje z widzem, wychodząc poza formułę ściśle instytucjonalnych pokazów i prezentacji, aneksuje przestrzeń miejską i poddaje ją artystycznym transformacjom. **ARTLOOP** to artystyczne laboratorium, które łączy młodą sztukę za sztuką uznaną, łącząc przestrzenie, idee i koncepcje, łączy ludzi, otwierając ich na nowe aktywności, konteksty, emocje.

Hasło
tegorocznej edycji
to **KUMULACJA**

To po pierwsze kumulacja doświadczeń nagromadzonych podczas dotychczasowych odsłon projektu, z których każda była inną próbą odczytania przestrzeni Sopotu poprzez interwencje artystów wizualnych, kino i przedsięwzięcia muzyczne. W tym roku, pragniemy spojrzeć od zewnątrz zarówno na sam festiwal, jak i na miasto, w którym się on rozgrywa.
Ten zewnętrzny punkt widzenia, umożliwiający krytyczny dystans – jednak bez opuszczania przestrzeni symbolicznej miasta – odnajdujemy na sopockim Molo. To właśnie ono jest miejscem, w którym ogniskujemy tegoroczną edycję **ARTLOOP** i kumulujemy artystyczne interpretacje oraz odczytania przestrzeni publicznej. Celem realizowanych w ramach festiwalu **ARTLOOP** działań, jest wplecenie w turystyczno-wypoczynkową narrację Molo alternatywnych wątków wprowadzonych przez interweniujących w tę wyjątkową przestrzeń artystów. Na Molo prowadzą wszystkie sopockie ścieżki; pragniemy aby w tym samym miejscu zbiegły się snute przez artystów nici krytycznej refleksji nad miastem, jego relacjami z morzem i rozwijającymi się na tle tych relacji rytuałami, zachowaniami i strukturami społecznymi.

Tematem przewodnim symbolicznej i urbanistycznej narracji Sopotu jest morze – jego brzeg, plaża, panorama, szum fali i daleki horyzont. Wszystkie drogi w Sopocie prowadzą nad morze. Molo jest kulminacją tego zainteresowania: miejską struktura, która przekracza brzeg i przenosi charakterystyczne dla Sopotu formy życia społecznego – wypoczynek, lans, autoreprezentacje, spacery, biznes turystyczny, uczestnictwo w spektaklu natury w roli widza – w głąb morza. Z drugiej strony Molo to jedyne miejsce w Sopocie, z którego spojrzeć można na samo miasto z pewnej perspektywy, ujrzeć je od zewnątrz. Wejście na Molo jest ruchem w kierunku morza i horyzontu, ale powrót z Mola jest ruchem w kierunku miasta. W ramach **ARTLOOP** pragniemy wykorzystać obydwa te wektory i podpowiadaną przez nie dwutorową refleksję na temat szczególnej kondycji nadmorskiego kurortu. Molo traktujemy jako miejsce, w którym dochodzi do kumulacji sopockiej tożsamości. Tu charakter przestrzeni publicznej Sopotu spełnia się ostatecznie. Dlatego właśnie na Molo – i w jego najbliższym otoczeniu – kumulujemy większość realizacji tegorocznego festiwalu.

Wystawie **KUMULACJA** towarzyszy program filmowy w formie wieloekranowej Kinoinstalacji w Państwowej Galerii Sztuki, lekcje mistrzowskie i spotkania z artystami oraz działania z zakresu designu miejskiego – obiekt "Kumulacja Marzeń" na Placu Przyjaciół Sopotu. Zapraszamy również do zabytkowej Willi na Goyki 3 w Sopocie, gdzie odbywa się projekt specjalny – druga odsłona "Wieży Ciśnień" Piotra Metza.

Koncepcję programową festiwalu opracował międzymiastowy [Sopot-Warszawa-Kraków] **Kolektyw Kuratorski** w składzie: **Lena Dula, Małgorzata Gołębiewska, Emilia Orzechowska, Ewa Szabłowska, Stach Szabłowski.**

Opisy poszczególnych
wydarzeń znajdują się
na stronie:

www.artloop.pl/program

ARTLOOP °5
FESTIVAL

ZAPROSZENIE

ARTLOOP °5
FESTIVAL

PROGRAM GODZINOWY

ARTLOOP °5
FESTIVAL

Prezydent Miasta Sopotu
oraz Dyrektor Państwowej Galerii Sztuki
w Sopocie
zapraszają na inauguracje wystawie
artystycznej

05 ARTLOOP FESTIVAL
pod hasłem
KUMULACJA

PAŃSTWOWA GALERIA SZTUKI

 PANTONE 286U + PANTONE 1788U

TEDxNingbo City Live

Design Studio: A piece of_Design Studio
Designers: Tseng Kuo Chan, I-Mei Lee
Client: TEDxNingbo

Visual identity designed for 2017 TedxNingbo annual event. Bold typography was used in gradient effect to create an overlooking angle of the city. The colour blue stands for the image of this coastal city, and red is the standard colour of TED event. Two-colour gradient effect also conveys the scenery that the city is constantly changing and thriving.

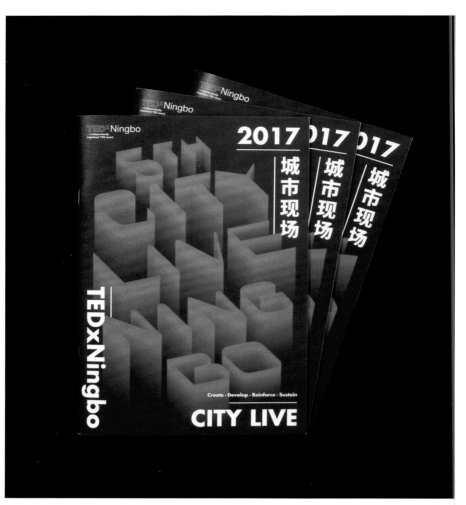

2017 MGGTW 3rd

Designer: Tseng Kuo Chan / *Client:* MGGTW

PANTONE 807C + PANTONE 286C

The poster design used the technique of inversive geometry and gradient shapes. The blurring effect represents that boundary of motion graphics and animation is being broken. For the printed poster, the designer used double-sided paper with only single-sided coating, in order to stress that motion graphics and animation are constantly being compared and discussed.

Fernet Branca. Único

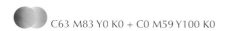 C63 M83 Y0 K0 + C0 M59 Y100 K0

Único para todos

Designer: Marcela M. Torres (rigelmoon)
Client: Fernet Branca

Único para todos was one of the 22 finalist posters in the 2017 Arte Unico Contest (Unique Art Contest) initiated by Fernet Branca. It was exhibited in the Amalia Fortabat Foundation and then in the rest of Argentina in a traveling exhibition. Here is the designer Marcela M. Torres's own interpretation of the poster: Oppressed by our own heads, and trying to ensure that each of our decisions is not submitted to the opinions of others, we live daily fed by pressure and chained to prejudice. At night, we share the tainted air of the bars, rolling up our sleeves to not loosen up this fight, and we ask for something refreshing to drink. Then, the waiter arrives, with a friendly smile and friendly treatment, and without hesitation, he gives the longed-for glass of fernet to our male companion. And it's there, my friend, in a small revolutionary act, you put all the prejudices down and you free yourself by saying: "Excuse me, the fernet is for me".

 C0 M100 Y0 K0 + C100 M0 Y0 K0

Resonant + Sundaze –
Visual Identity

Design Studio: Due Collective
Creative Directors: Alessio Pompadura, Massimiliano Vitti
Designers: Alessio Pompadura, Massimiliano Vitti
Client: Resonant

Resonant is a brand that promotes and manages events related to the local electronic music world. The design research goes deep into the study of the cymatics and its principles. Every sound impulse is matched by a specific design, a generative identity that draws different shapes by rotating and moving typeface modules inside a square grid.

Sundaze is the first Resonant event, a 24 hrs pool party. The communication of the event merges the Resonant identity concept with the effect of light refraction and object distortion through water. The typography becomes visual and deforms itself as if it were immersed in the pool. The selected colour palette is composed of pure magenta and pure cyan, two saturated and vibrant colours that have allowed a consistent colour rendering between digital and printing communication.

⊙ 5am

05/24

⊙ 6am

06/24

C99 M95 Y4 K0 + C1 M81 Y56 K0

C0 M85 Y35 K0 + C2 M13 Y55 K0

C65 M56 Y1 K0 + C3 M1 Y17 K0

C80 M61 Y0 K0 + C4 M21 Y58 K0

C71 M39 Y0 K0 + C0 M2 Y15 K0

C80 M61 Y0 K0 + C2 M39 Y61 K0

C98 M93 Y0 K4 + C2 M96 Y79 K8

Time in Colour

Designer: Tom Anders Watkins

This sets of posters are designer's exploration of the relationship between time and colour. According to new research, colour is a reliable sensory way of telling time. The designer sets out to explore what every hour within a day actually looks like. There are 24 posters in the series, using gradients and the linear angles of a traditional clock.

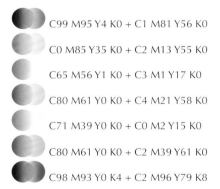

⊖ 3pm

15/24

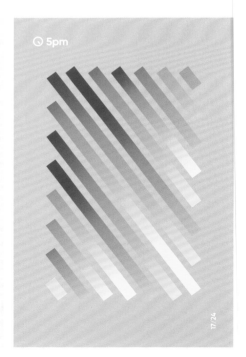

⊙ 5pm

17/24

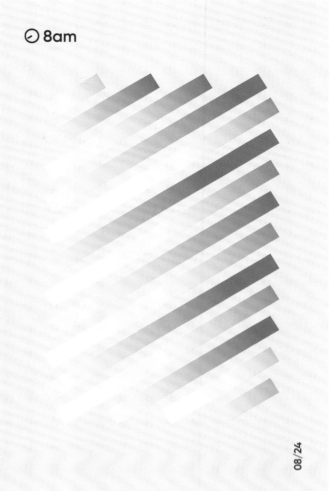

Silkscreen printing
in single-coloured paper + one paint

Innovation

Design Studio: Saatchi & Saatchi IS
Creative Director: Rafał Nagiecki
Designer: Anna Caban- Szypenbeil
3D Artists/Animators:
Anna Caban-Szypenbeil, Bartosz Morawski
Design Supporters:
Albert Krajewski, Artur Herc, Katarzyna Góźdź
Client: Stowarzyszenie Komunikacji Marketingowej

Posters were designed for Innovation, an unique event, conference and competition that addresses and defines the need of groundbreaking solutions and innovative approach in the field of advertising, start-ups and e-commerce. But every creative solution needs a certain amount of mistakes that moves the comfort zone a little further. That's why the designers decided to use the glitch effect to achieve visual distortion to create non-obvious objects and leave more space for imagination. The glitch effect also enables them to create some optical illusions in animations too. Posters were made in silkscreen technique, which gave them opportunity to create a variety of colour versions of prints in very short series.

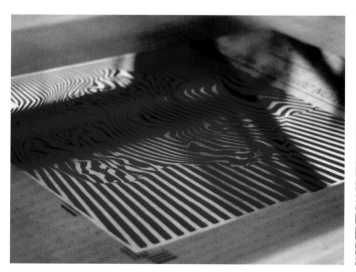

DARE TO ABANDON YOUR COMFORT ZONE

FORUM INNOVATION 2017 24-25 KWIETNIA

1 DZIEŃ 24.04:
- Otwarcie FORUM
- Wręczenie nagród
- Networking

2 DZIEŃ 25.04:
- Prelekcje
- Startup Speed Dates

STUDIO BIAŁE
UL. MIŃSKA 65, WARSZAWA
WWW.INNOVATION.SAR.ORG.PL

ORGANIZATOR

sar:
STOWARZYSZENIE
KOMUNIKACJI
MARKETINGOWEJ

SPONSORZY

PARTNERZY

PATRONI MEDIALNI

AUDYTOR

PRODUKCJA

 PANTONE 286 C + PANTONE 806 C

Tame Impala
Screen Print

Designer: Rhianne Connelly

A series of limited edition screen prints created for an exhibition of posters inspired by music, musicians and music culture. Choosing to focus on the song *Let It Happen* by Tame Impala, the designer Rhianne Connelly interpreted their distinctive sound of psychedelic rock by creating a bold geometric pattern. A halftone texture was then applied to this, adding a more subtle detail to the finished print. Drawing on their psychedelic influences, the impact of this design really comes alive with the introduction of two vibrant and contrasting colours. These posters were hand printed using the split fountain method with fluorescent pink and ultramarine ink. Keeping a stripped back palette with this particular printing technique allowed the designer to experiment with the stock she was printing on, giving the inks something more playful to stand out against. The split fountain method mixes her chosen inks as they are pulled across the screen, which makes each screen print truly unique.

INDEX

Ares Pedroli

Ares Pedroli graduated from the School for Artistic Industries at Lugano, Switzerland. He specializes in graphic design and is now an independent designer.

http://arespedroli.ch/
P168-169

Acrobat WiseFull

Gdańsk-based creative studio Acrobat WiseFull prides itself in its ability to meet their clients' expectations with the help of their self-titled acrobatic skills – flexible approach and unconventional ways of thinking, fittingly calling it the balancing act of creative work. Working for numerous clients far and near, Acrobat WiseFull's clear vision and broad skill set has earned them the trust of their clients, as well as numerous honorary mentions and awards.

www.acrobat.com.pl
P032

Adelia Lim

Adelia is a freelance graphic designer based in Singapore who is inquisitive in nature. In any design project, she values the process as much as the final outcome. She is always interested in finding alternative, yet equally valid ways of representing information. At the heart of it, it has been an on-going journey for her in understanding what graphic design is and the role it plays in shaping perceptions.

https://adelia-lim.info
P214-215

Aksion Ivankov

Aksion Ivankov is a graphic designer with over three years of work experience and Art-director of Extreme Style organization. Now he is based in Sumy, Ukraine. One of his works was selected as the winner of the city competition. He specializes in branding, identity, packaging and illustrations. And nowadays he is also working with many social projects, like Sumy Extreme Style festival.

www.chokolad.com.ua
P170-171

Anna Caban-Szypenbeil

Anna Caban-Szypenbeil is a 3D designer based in Warsaw. She focuses on 3D illustration and animation. Together with Saatchi & Saatchi IS team, she designed posters for Innovation conference.

http://annacaban.pl/
P230-231

Attila Hadnagy

Attila is a London based multi-disciplinary graphic designer and creative with more than 5 years experience in the design industry. He is the founder of Brandimension. His work ranges from logo design, branding, illustration to print and packaging design. Attila has worked with clients and brands all around the world.

www.brandimension.com
P056-057

azul recreo

azul recreo is a graphic design studio based in Madrid, founded by Mateo Buitrago and Elisa Piquer. Their work is characterized by the active role of illustration in most of their projects. They understand it as a powerful way to humanize, simplify complex things and connect people to their childish side. They love designing and playing with illustration to build visual languages, create brands or develop ideas.

http://azulrecreo.com
P050-051

Bardo Industries

Bardo Industries is an independent cross-disciplinary design studio based in Brooklyn, New York. From global brands to small businesses, they take every project with the same passion and commitment, working together with clients to create long-lasting design solutions. Their approach is built on conceptual thinking, research, and collaboration, to develop clear and transformative interactive brand experiences across multiple platforms. Bardo is a woman-owned business.

www.bardoind.com
P044-045

Beatrice Bianchet, Gloria Maggioli

Beatrice and Gloria are two friends and freelancers who love typography and books. They met in 2014 at ISIA Urbino, the most important Graphic Design and Visual Communication Institute in Italy. Now they are working in Milan and Turin.

www.behance.net/beatricebianchet
www.behance.net/GloriaMaggioli
P204-205

Belen Ramos

Belen is a designer from Argentina currently living in Australia. She has a passion for crafted typography and refined colour palettes. Her approach to design is vibrant and bold — with conceptual thinking and attention to detail at the core of everything she does. While her career began in advertising agencies and design studios, today she works as a freelance designer providing a specialised service primarily in the areas of branding, editorial design and packaging.

www.belenramos.com
P024-025

Blok Design

Blok Design is founded in 1998. They have been collaborating with thinkers and creators, companies and brands, from all over the world, taking on projects that blend cultural awareness, their love of art, and their belief in humanity to advance society and business alike. No matter what projects they take on, the studio's intent is to create indelible experiences that profoundly affect people and in some way help expand their understanding of the world around them.

http://blokdesign.com
P068-069, P130-131

Bocanegra Studio

Bocanegra is a small independent Italian studio. They create brand identities for all types of companies, both large and small, finding effective, smart and timeless solutions.

http://bocanegrastudio.com
P060-061, P144-147

Brand Unit

Brand Unit is a Vienna based network for branding, design and content established in 2011 by Albert Handler, Andreas Oberkanins and Ulrike Tschabitzer-Handler. They are a unit of joint forces from different walks of business-life, pooling their experience, know-how and training in strategy, branding, business development, communication, project management, design and photography, to help the brand find the right solution.

www.brand-unit.com
P148-149

Brandon Fretwell

Brandon is a multidisciplinary designer currently finishing his last year at California State University, the USA. He is working in digital and print design, brand identity, and interactive experiences. He has a passion for work that shares a good match between communication and design. He started designing after getting out of the United States Army and since then he has had the opportunity to learn disciplines in graphic design, branding, art direction, sustainable design, front end development, packaging, and user experience and interface.

www.brandonfretwell.com
P038-039

Brodie Kaman

Brodie is a 25 year old freelance graphic designer and artist from Perth, Australia currently living and working in London. Choosing projects that resonate with him, he takes an experimental, DIY approach to his work.

http://brodiekaman.com/
P104-105

Chen, Hao-En

Chen, Hao-En is a graphic designer based in Taiwan who is obsessed and passionate about creating beautiful things, but also enjoys in their own design fantasy creation. His design inspirations mostly come from his life experiences. He insists on jumping off the frame, communicating through design to discover more possibilities for design.

www.behance.net/haoenchen
P070

Chieh-Ting Lee

Born in 1991, Chieh-Ting majored in graphic design and is now doing research in attractiveness of picture and typography.

www.behance.net/leechiehting
P216-217

Chiun Hau You

Chiun Hau You is a student studying at the Department of Design in Taiwan Tech. He also works as an independent graphic designer and web developer. He focuses on branding, visual, packaging, UI design, and web-based interactive technologies.

www.behance.net/chiunhauyou
P029-030

Chiwai Cheang

Chiwai graduated from NYUST and started his studio SomethingMoon Design in 2011. Now he is based in Macau and often works for the local cultural and arts groups, and has been the recipient of numerous local and international design awards.

https://somethingmoon.com
P184-185

Chris Do

Chris Do is an Emmy award winning director, designer, strategist and educator. He is the Chief Strategist and CEO of Blind, executive producer of The Skool, and the Founder of The Futur— an online education platform that teaches the business of design to creative thinkers. Founded in 1995, Blind has been a pioneer in the motion design field and has made hundreds of award-winning commercials, music videos and broadcast promos that combine design, typography, animation, live action and visual effects for screens and clients of all sizes.

www.behance.net/chrisdo
P027

Coletivo Plomo71

Coletivo Plomo71 is a collaboration between four designers who share the same interest in typography. Together, they develop professional and personal projects including visual identity, lettering, calligraphy, illustration, editorial design and font development. They believe what guarantees the quality of the results is the involvement in the process, so their project vision naturally permeates through manual and digital media.

www.plomo71.com
P136

Cristian Robles

Cristian is a freelance illustrator from Spain, Barcelona.

www.behance.net/kensausage
P034-035

Curtis Rayment

Curtis Rayment is a multidisciplinary Graphic Designer from the South Coast of England. Influenced by all things physically engaging, his approach leads him to a process-driven practice that focuses on the translation of behaviours through design.

www.curtisrayment.co.uk
P150-151

Dacil Sánchez

Dacil Sánchez is a graphic designer based in Bilbao, Spain. Most of the time she works on designing visual identities and web pages, but her true passion is designing for social purposes and issues.

www.behance.net/dacil_sanchez
P076-077

Dmitry Neal

Russian designer Dmitry Neal specializes in branding and interior design for bars and restaurants, giving preferences to loft and Scandinavian styles. He appreciates natural materials and contrasting combinations of textures and interior items.

http://dmitryneal.ru
P040-041

Due Collective

Due is a graphic design collective born in November 2016 in Perugia, Italy. Co-founded by Alessio Pompadura and Massimiliano Vitti, they design communication systems for commercial, cultural and artistic fields. They focus on print, visual identity, editorial design and typography.

www.behance.net/du-e
P226-227

Dulce Cruz

Dulce is a designer based in Porto, Portugal. After ten years of working in big advertising and design agencies, she is now a freelancer specialized in packaging, editorial design and small special editions. She prefers projects where she is able to focus on the story and create non obvious connections creating unique narrative and visual effect rather than worrying about mass commercial objectives or selling points.

http://cargocollective.com/dulcecruz
P122-123

Ediciones El Fuerte

Ediciones El Fuerte is a small publisher project from Buenos Aires that makes zines and posters using Risograph and etching. Based on illustration, graphic story, abstraction, and concepts about science, travel, cosmos, cultures, obsessions, they make zines and graphic work investigating different printing techniques, where the analog and the handcraft are the main characters. Even if El Fuerte is a young project they already have been in several fairs in Buenos Aires, Santiago de Chile and London.

www.edicioneselfuerte.tumblr.com
P158-159

Estudio Machete

Machete is a design studio based in Bogotá, Colombia, created in 2013 by Alejandro Mancera and Diego García, both of them are artists. Laura Cárdenas and Laura Daza joined the team later on. Estudio Machete is focused on the development of editorial projects as a whole. They are inspired by the communication design and are always looking for reaching the sensitivity needed for its construction.

www.estudiomachete.com
P186-187

Evan Wijaya

Evan Wijaya is a Jakarta-based graphic designer specialising in branding, illustration, and editorial design. He is also passionate about graphic design for films as well as film production design. Evan graduated in Visual Communication Design from Universitas Pelita Harapan in 2017. He is fascinated by things that are related to history, culture, astronomy, and fiction/fantasy. Those combined become the inspiration for his works and influence him a lot. He is interested in conceptual design that stretches across mediums and puts high attention to details.

www.evanwijaya.com
P052-053, P082-083

Explicit Design Studio

Explicit Design Studio is a Budapest-based Hungarian creative studio specialized in graphic/web/UI/UX design, typography, branding, editorial design, photo and video making. The team is always open to new connections and possibilities, for this reason the working process is quick and effective. The continually extending design studio has currently four members: Hunor Kátay, Sebestyén Németh, Szilárd Kovács and Márton Ács.

http://explicitstudio.hu/
P192-193

Familia

Familia is a Barcelona based graphic design studio that works with groups of typefaces, colours, materials, formats, solutions and people, with experience in the fields of graphic identity, editorial design, packaging, website and apps. They think about design in a holistic way, and they believe in complete, coherent and consistent graphic solutions adapted to the specific needs of each project—solutions that serve as a graphic vehicle to help their customers structure and identify themselves.

www.byfamilia.com
P062-063, P085, P096-097

Fast, Liang

Fast, Liang is a young designer based in Taiwan. His works range from graphic design, editorial design, typography design to communication materials and identity design.

www.behance.net/fastliang
P036-037

Formdusche

Formdusche is active in the broad field of communications design. Ever since its inception in 2004, Formdusche's main goal, plain and simple, has been to conceive individual answers for each client's tasks. Both dictums, listen to the client and form follows content, rank on top of their design philosophy charts. As their work is concept-driven, they like to irritate with typographic ideas or to find simple solutions for complex processes.

www.formdusche.de
P046, P120-121

Gauthier

Gauthier helps the brand to make sound marketing-communications decisions. They create forceful, coherent messages that are relevant to the success of the brand, whether it is a product, a service or an idea. Gauthier offers their clients uncommon flexibility in deliverables and timelines, based on over 25 years of experience and on strengths they value, including proficiency in complex issues, a collaborative approach and consistent quality of execution.

http://gauthierdesigners.com
P014-015, P080-081

Gruta Design

The Gruta Design studio is a creative den where ideas merge, generating new perspectives to perceive the world. It works with an innovative look exploring and experiencing the ways that design provides in search of creative solutions.

www.behance.net/grutadesign
P090

Heitor Kimura

Heitor is a Brazilian graphic artist, who is colorblind and a philosophy lover.

www.behance.net/heitorkim
P126-127

Isabel Beltrán, Pamela Sada

Isabel and Pamela are two designers from Mexico who work in collaboration for different editorial design and branding projects.

www.behance.net/isabeltranb
www.behance.net/pamsada
P178

Jaemin Lee

Graphic Designer Jaemin Lee graduated from Seoul National University and founded studio fnt in 2006. He took part in several exhibitions and worked with clients like National Museum of Contemporary Art, Seoul Museum of Art, National Theater Company of Korea and Seoul Records & CD Fair Organizing Committee on many cultural events and concerts. Since 2011, he has actively worked with Junglim Foundation on projects about architecture, culture, arts and education, forum, exhibitions and research in order to explore meaningful exchanges with the public about subjects like the social role of architecture and urban living. He also teaches graphic design at Seoul National University and University of Seoul. He is an AGI (Alliance Graphique Internationale) member since 2016.

www.leejaemin.net
P084, P094-095, P179

Jihye Kim

Jihye graduated from Seoul Women's University in Seoul, South Korea and she currently works as a graphic design freelancer in Seoul.

www.behance.net/57kimjihye
P135

Jim Wong

Hong Kong graphic designer Jim Wong co-founded Good Morning Design, specializes in visual identity, prints and publication. Jim has been actively participated in various exhibitions, workshops and sharings. His works have been selected for numerous design awards including D&AD and German Design Award, and published in design magazines and publications internationally.

www.gd-morning.org/jim
P066-067

John Dias dos Santos

John Dias dos Santos is an Art Director with more than 15 years of experience, based in Brazil.

https://dropr.com/johndias
www.behance.net/jdsanbr
P088-089

Justin Kemerling

Justin Kemerling is an independent designer, activist, and collaborator living in Nebraska, the USA, focused on making it beautiful, moving people to action, and getting good things done. He works primarily with community organizations, political campaigns, and changemaking startups in need of branding, graphic design, web design, and art direction. His self-initiated projects and collaborations explore ways to move forward important causes and ideas with design, art, and other forms of creative expression.

www.justinkemerling.com
P020-021

Justyna Radziej

Justyna is a graphic designer and visual artist, graduated from Academy of Fine Arts in Łódź, Poland. She specializes in visual identity for cultural events, brand identity design and editorial design. Graphic and print are her passion for over ten years. She seeks to use old printing techniques – from silkscreen to letterpress – in her professional and artistic works.

https://www.behance.net/JustynaRadziej
P032, P042-043

K95

K95 is a digital creative agency based in Catania, Italy, originating from the passion of a group of friends skilled in graphic and typography.

www.k95.it
P128-129, P176-177

Kebba Sanneh

The Parisian artist Kebba Sanneh works as an Illustrator and Art Director since 2005. With a very personal style, he mixes pointillism, surrealism and collage. Kebba has really created a unique, fantastical, sometimes dark and off-beat universe.

http://kebba.fr
P072-073

Kevin Brenkman, Bibi Kelder, Tijn Bakker

Kevin Brenkman, Bibi Kelder and Tijn Bakker are students at LUCA School of the Arts, in Ghent, Belgium.

http://kevinbrenkman.com
https://itsmebibi.nl
http://www.tijnbakker.com
P064-065

Kötöde

"Kötöde" is an acronym of three Hungarian phrases, binding, typesetting and design. The team is a study group of the Hungarian University of Fine Arts.

www.behance.net/kotode
P124-125

Laura Cárdenas

Laura Cárdenas is a Colombian graphic designer. She is interested in editorial and data design, and she also works with big scale typography in a design collective named "Type of tape".

www.behance.net/lauracardenasa
P018-019, P186-187

Le Séisme

Le Séisme is an independant design studio in Montreal.

http://leseisme.com
P026

Ledoux Mélissa

Curious and sparkling French Graphic Design student, Melissa loves to work with colours and textures. Always ready to learn or try something new, she just wants to mix everything she knows to create something unexpected.

www.behance.net/melissaled74e1
P086-087

Les produits de l'épicerie

Created in 2003, Les produits de l'épicerie aspires to excite people's imagination with their graphic and photographic images. The creative trio (Jérôme Grimbert / Philippe Delforge / Marieke Offroy) work in the field of art, music and architecture, with particular attention to creating powerful visual and touches in the end results.

www.lesproduitsdelepicerie.org
P142, P167, P174-175

Lucia Rossetti

Lucia Rossetti is a recent Graphic Design graduate from Sheffield Hallam Institute of Arts. Lucia's portfolio is eclectic from experimenting with typography to art direction and advertising.

www.behance.net/LuciaRossetti
P134

Lully Duque

Lully Duque is a graphic designer and art director based in Bogotá, Colombia. She is interested in art, culture and the development of visual communication. She specializes in visual identity and branding. In the last two years, she has also been involved in urban art projects that combine her skills in graphic design, typography and tape art to create unique installations and visual pieces.

www.behance.net/lullyduque
P202-203

Marcela M. Torres (rigelmoon)

Marcela graduated from Graphic Design program at Universidad de Buenos Aires, and she has been working as an Art Director in advertising industry for more than 10 years. Her technical and academic training, plus her design, creativity, and art experience inspired her to find a new ludic path to mix and match all those disciplines. That interest and desire took her to illustration.

www.rigelmoon.com.ar
P225

Marcell Kazsik

Marcell is a Hungarian graphic artist and designer, based in Budapest, and currently studying at the Hungarian University of Fine Arts.

http://kazsik.com
P200-201

Mariana Gabardo

Mariana is a Brazilian graphic designer and art director currently living and working in Porto Alegre, south of Brazil. She has experience working in diverse fields of graphic design, ranging from art direction, digital projects and branding. Her services include branding, identity, packaging, concept creation, web & mobile projects, editorial design, UX and social media.

www.behance.net/mariegabardo
P116-117

Marina Cardoso

As a freelance graphic designer, over the past two years Marina has been thriving a path of experimenting different techniques over print, digital and mixed media supports. From pencil drawings, to linocuts, screen prints, stamps, embroidery, paint and several other mediums, she intends to yield different projects day after day. With a constant will of communicating some of her routine facts and favorite extracts, such as movies, records, books and exhibitions, Marina keeps engaged in the feminist cause and relates to indie-emo-punk-shoegaze-synthpop movements.

www.behance.net/cardosomarina
P137

Marine Laurent

Marine Laurent is a french graphic designer and illustrator. Her visual universe is built around the world of childhood, the current graphic creation and her attraction to manual practices, such as Risograph printing. The image, and more generally the graphic design, is for her a vast universe of research and experimentation. She loves working with digital tools as well as with her hands.

www.marinelaurent.com
P143, P166

Marisol De la Rosa Lizárraga

Marisol is a graphic designer from Monterrey, Mexico, who is passionate about editorial design, illustration and lettering.

www.behance.net/marisoldel963d
P132-133

Marta Gawin

Marta Gawin (born in 1985, Poland) is a multidisciplinary graphic designer specialized in visual identity, communication and editorial design. Since her MA in Graphic Design (Academy of Fine Arts, Katowice) in 2011, she has been working as a freelancer for cultural institutions and commercial organizations. Her design approach is conceptual, logical and content-driven. She treats graphic design as a field of visual research and formal experiments.

www.gawin.design
P100-101, P180-181

Martin Dupuis

Martin Dupuis is a Montreal-based art director with a background in cinema, fine art, illustration and graphic design. He currently works at Les Évadés.

www.rightearleft.com/
P034-035

Mary Vinogradova

Mary Vinogradova is a young graphic designer based in Ukraine. She specializes in brand identity, editorial design and packaging. She is fond of silk-screen printing and works with the form. She is the winner of ADC*UA Awards (Young and Students) 2017.

www.behance.net/marivin
P028

Mathieu Delestre

Mathieu is a Paris-based multidisciplinary freelance designer specializing in print and digital graphic identity since 2005 and works mostly in the luxury and cultural sectors. The different facets of his work cover a wide spectrum of styles and graphic universes, allowing him to evolve in many areas such as graphic identity, illustration, layout or collage.

http://buroneko.com/
P072-073

Mercedes Bazan

Mercedes is a graphic designer from Buenos Aires, Argentina. She studied at the University of Buenos Aires (UBA). She worked in different design agencies and recently moved to San Francisco to join Stripe.

www.mechibazan.com
P108-109

Merkitys

Merkitys is a design studio based in Helsinki, Finland. They develop meaningful brands and strong visual identities with clients of all sizes. They aim at creating holistic, purposeful and exciting design solutions for small and big companies, organizations and public agencies. Their work is a mixture of deep strategic know-how and uncompromising attention to quality.

www.merkitys.eu
P194-195

Michelangelo Greco

Michelangelo is a graphic design student at the last year at the Academy of Fine Arts in Bologna, Italy. He has been carrying out his research for about ten years now, colour is and has always been a focal point of his research.

www.behance.net/dudegraph643e
P031

Moving Studio

Moving Studio is a Graphic Design, 3D and Motion Graphics agency. They add value to brands through unique, quality focused design that builds audiences, changes perceptions and enhances business.

www.movingstudio.co.uk/
P110-111

Natalya Balnova

Natalya Balnova is a New York based illustrator, designer and printmaker. She graduated from the MFA Illustration as Visual Essay program at the School of Visual Arts, received a BFA in Communication Arts from the Parsons School of Design, as well as a BFA in Communication Arts from the Academy of Industrial Art and Design (St Petersburg, Russia). She has been recognized by American Illustration, The Society of Illustrators, Print Design Annual, Art Directors Club, 3x3 Magazine, Creative Quarterly, Art Book Wanted.

www.natalyabalnova.com
P156-157

Nova Iskra Studio

Nova Iskra Studio is a consulting and design studio that offers creative solutions from the field of branding, print, digital innovation and architecture using human-centered design methodology to create new solutions that are tailor-made to suit people's needs.

www.novaiskrastudio.com
P078-079

O Hezin

O Hezin is a graphic designer who is based in Seoul. She runs a graphic design studio OYE, working primarily in the cultural field on graphic design, illustration and publishing projects.

www.o-y-e.kr
P102-103

O.OO Risograph & Design Room

Formed by two graphic designers, O.OO is a design studio based in Taiwan. Since opening, they have been offering Design and Risograph printing solutions. They believe that with every new project or challenge, they can uncover solutions, and discover the possibilities of Design and Risograph printing.

www.odotoo.com
P196-197

Onion Design Associates

Onion Design Associates is a multi-disciplinary design studio in Taiwan. Their work on the album "Formosa Medicine Show" was nominated for Best Album Packaging at the 57th Grammy Awards and 25th Golden melody Award. They have been also honored by numerous awards, including DFA (Design For Asia award), Golden Pin Award, SDA Shopping Design Award Best 100, HKDA Global Design Award and selected by Tokyo TDC Awards. Their work has also been featured in various international publications.

www.oniondesign.com.tw
P138-139

Onss Mhirsi

Onss is a young graphic designer specialized in both print and digital design with particular interest in branding and editorial design. She is passionate about building cohesive and strong brands as well as typography and packaging. Hard working and enthusiastic, she is a compulsive collector of restaurant menus and packages.

www.behance.net/onssmhirsi
P074-075

Openmint

Openmint is an international branding and design studio working all around the world. They enjoy working with people who share their values — people who are open-minded and passionate about what they do. Their clients are responsible and reveal conscious approach to the way they live, behave and work. Openmint is a family design studio founded by designers Dmitry Zhelnov and Katerina Teterkina.

www.behance.net/openmint
P054-055

Pelo

Pelo is an Italian zine founded by a collective of illustrators that in every issue deals with an irreverent topic, outspokenly. Through PELO, they have set the goal of working with contributing illustrators who share their philosophy and producing a creative space where exciting, innovative, and knowledgeable work thrives. They believe this is the opportunity to freely produce something together while also having fun, in order to establish a direct dialogue based on irony with the public.

www.pelomagazine.com/
P164-165

Qingyu Wu

Qingyu Wu (Q) is a graphic designer, krautrock lover based in New York City. Qingyu holds a BFA in Graphic Design from Virginia Commonwealth University and an MFA in 2D Design from Cranbrook Academy of Art. Her work has a focus on printed matter and graphic identities. Clients range from independent artists, musicians to brands, schools, and museums. Her work has been recognized by the American Institute of Graphic Arts (AIGA), the Type Directors Club (TDC), and China Graphic Design Association (CGDA), and was featured by AIGA Eye on Design, It's Nice That, People of Print, Ficciones Typografika, Women of Graphic Design and more. She was selected as one of the best graduate design student in 2017 by AIGA NY. Qingyu received the Gold Award from CGDA 2017 Graphic Design Academy Award and Certificates of Typographic Excellence Award from TDC 64. She has lectured at the Art Center College of Design, Parsons School of Design, and Pratt Institute.

https://qingyuwu.com/
P091

qu'est-ce que c'est design

qu'est-ce que c'est design is a graphic design studio that loves transforming ideas into compelling concepts and expressive graphic design. "What is it?—a simple question born out of necessity, with curiosity being the impetus of creation. The question is uncomplicated, but begs only for an answer that appropriately satisfies, among a million others. This, in its singularity, is what the Studio does.

www.quest-ce.com
P152-153, P162-163

Rhianne Connelly

Rhianne is a Scottish designer and printmaker, originally from Dundee and now working in London as a graphic designer. She is drawn to bold patterns, playful typography and print design. She is always looking to explore more tactile processes within her work such as hand-lettering and screen printing. As a designer, she enjoys the organic process of screen printing and the sometimes unpredictable nature of her printing journey. She sees the design process as a craft and she creates crafted graphic design.

www.behance.net/rhianneconnelly
P232

Ritter Willy Putra, Hendri Siman Santosa, Utari Kennedy, Edwin

A group of graphic designers who graduated from the same university – Multimedia Nusantara University, that now each works in a different graphic design studio in Jakarta and Tangerang, Indonesia.

www.behance.net/ritterwp
www.behance.net/utarikennedy
www.behance.net/bluekosa
www.behance.net/udnhz
P188-189

Robert Bazaev

Robert Bazaev is a Vladikavkaz based multidisciplinary graphic designer and art director, specializing in branding, packaging, motion design. His expertise lies in design, direction and ideas. The colour plays an important role in every project he does. He loves typography and connections between music and visuals, and that is reflected in his work.

http://robertbazaev.com/
P058-059

Roots

Roots is an independent branding & creative design studio, with keen focus on observing, understanding, and developing meaningful design stories for brands and businesses. The studio's works span across the fields of brand identity, print, book, exhibition and website. Roots is founded in 2011 and led by Jonathan Yuen, an established and recognised multi-disciplinary designer with over a decade of experience.

www.whererootsare.com
P190-191

Shanti Sparrow

Shanti Sparrow is an award winning Australian designer, illustrator and dreamer living and creating in New York. Sparrow has a vibrant and bold approach to design. She creates brands filled with individuality and personality. Her expressive typography and confident colour palettes create memorable and iconic branding.

www.shantisparrow.com
P006-008, P118-119

Song Ho Jong

Song Ho Jong is a graphic designer and advertising designer from Seoul, Korea. He studied advertising design in Seoil College, and now is working at Pentabreed company. He specializes in a variety of design disciplines and has advanced skills in using colours. He loves hiphop Music, Marvel and colours.

www.behance.net/ax_
P208-213

Stéphanie Triballier

Born in 1985, Stéphanie settles down in Rennes and joins the graphic garden in 2011. Since 2016, she works both in Rennes and Lorient, developing relationships and miscellaneous collaborations.
Her graphic writing is lively and coloured; the idea of movement and interactions between the materials, the illustrated subjects and the typography is the heart of her creation and thinking. As she is particularly sensitive to young public and to meditation work, she is extremely aware of real and practical issues. She occasionally provides services for academic workshops, but also for institutions and juries, such as ESAM, ESAC, ESADHaR, EESAB.

www.lejardingraphique.com
P098-099

Studio fnt

Studio fnt is a Seoul based graphic design studio that works on prints, identities, interactive/digital media and more. It collects fragmented and straying thoughts, and then organises and transforms them into relevant forms.

www.studiofnt.com
P094-095, P179

Studio Lennarts & de Bruijn

Lennarts & de Bruijn is a multidisciplinary Design Studio, based in The Hague, founded by Max Lennarts and Menno de Bruijn. The studio specializes in the following design disciplines, including identities, campaigns, concepts, copywriting, videos, websites, books, posters, branding, animations, exhibitions, illustrations, flyers, and more.

www.lennartsendebruijn.com
P012-013, P092-093

Thitipol Chaimattayompol

Thitipol is a graphic and packaging designer who currently attended a graduate program MS packaging design at Pratt Institute, NY. He has 2-year graphic design background working in the food industry in Thailand. He loves exploring new ideas and design as well as experimenting with colours and typefaces. Uniqueness and completeness are his primary design principle.

www.behance.net/northpolecb4c5
P172-173

Ti-Ming Chu

Ti-Ming Chu had an interest in drawing since a young age. After his graduation from Department of Communications Design at Shih Chien University, he was sure it was his destiny to be a designer. Creating masterpieces was not his ambition, and he just wishes to be true and make design of his own style. His long-time heroes include John Lennon, Bruce Lee and Stephen Chow.

www.timingchu.com
P071

Tom Anders Watkins

Tom is a half Finnish half English self-taught Designer / Film-Maker /Illustrator / Art Director. He currently works in London, freelancing in many creative disciplines.

www.tomanders.com
P228-229

Tomorrow Design Office

Tomorrow Design Office is a Hong Kong based graphic design studio started from 2013, aimed at creating simple, but practical and innovative design solutions that can influence the society and build a better tomorrow. They try to merge traditional intelligence and modern beauty, Chinese culture and Western execution to convey their own style, vision and direction. Their expertise lies in brand identity, visual communication, packaging, company brochure and marketing collateral.

www.tomorrowdesign.hk
P140-141

Toormix

Toormix was created in 2000 in Barcelona by Ferran Mitjans and Oriol Armengou. The studio uses creative thinking and design to generate innovative brand experiences through physical, digital or environmental media with a clear focus on the needs of the user, as well as an understanding of the business challenges and objectives. Their background and portfolio, the conferences, the workshops that they are invited to give in different countries and their teaching work in several design schools endorse their professional career.

www.toormix.com
P022-023

Tseng Kuo Chan

Tseng Kuo Chan is a graphic designer based in Taiwan. Works have been included in viction: ary, Design360 ° magazines and other Asian Pacific Design Yearbooks, recently selected for 2016 posters Mexico Poster Biennale (14th BICM). He currently works as a freelancer, specializing in Graphic Design, including CIS, VI, Branding, Book Cover, Magazine Layout, art and cultural performance, exhibition's identity design.

www.behance.net/tsengreen
P154-155, P222-223, P224

Tun Ho

Tun Ho is a graphic designer now based in Macau. He dabbles in graphic design and illustrations.

www.behance.net/tunho
www.imtunho.com
P048-049

Uniforma

Uniforma is a creative studio founded in 2007 by Michał Mierzwa. They operate in various fields of visual communication using a wide range of digital technologies, often collaborating with other designers.

www.uniforma.pl
P220-221

Verena Hsieh, Zora Wu, Karen Chang, Sharmaine Liu

These four talents are classmates studying at Fu Jen Catholic University, Taiwan. Their major is Applied Art with an emphasis on Visual Communication. Verena and Sharmaine are the head of the overall concept; Zora and Karen are in charge of graphic design.

www.behance.net/b83090184b4
www.behance.net/Zora_Wu
www.behance.net/weichun
www.behance.net/bb22670
P016-017

Vetro Design

Vetro Design is a leading design agency based in Collingwood, Melbourne with a simple philosophy: to create outstanding design solutions that add value to their client's bottom line. They provide exceptional creative outcomes that enable their clients to communicate the products and/or services to the target market. They are branding specialists with a wealth of experience working with small to medium business as well as local and state government, helping to create and build brands across a wide range of communication outcomes including print, digital and environment.

www.vetro.com.au
P112-113

Vladimir Garbo

Vladimir Garboš is an architect and graphic designer from Zrenjanin, Serbia. He received his formal education as an architect, but graphic design (and design in general) was a great interest and passion also. He works mostly on the projects which interact with culture and art, being also involved in exhibition design, stage and light design with governmental institutions and non-governmental organizations.

www.behance.net/vldmr
P114-115

W/H Design Studio

W/H Ltd. is an experienced, creative and passionate group of designers, developers, and project managers. The company specializes in branding, graphic and interior design, CIS, and integrated design in a contextual cross field. Every client they work with becomes a part of the team. Together they face the challenges, develop a set of design, and integrate service solution.
Their mission is to help their clients make distinctive, innovative, and substantial improvements in their industry. They provide an integrated design service solution that includes graphic design, web design and management, digital marketing, e-commerce, exhibition planning and design services.

www.whdesignstudio.com
P198-199

WANG2MU

WANG2MU is an independent designer and artist based in Shanghai, China.

www.behance.net/wang2mu
P033

Whitney Bolin, Axel Vagnard

Whitney Bolin and Axel Vagnard are independent art directors based in Paris, France. The American-French duo teamed their design skills during their studies at Penninghen where they both obtained their master's degrees in Art Direction. Combining Whitney's keen eye for colour and form with Axel's intuitive knack for typography and details, they're passionate about solving creative challenges with original, personal solutions.

www.behance.net/whitneybolin
www.behance.net/axelvagnar365d
P218-219

Youvi. Chow

As a young visual designer and an illustrator born in 1992, based in Shanghai, China, Youvi pays close attention on digital art, exhibition design, brand identity, illustration, and editorial design. Her design works have been selected by PLAYBOY design competition and ADCK, also attended exhibition in Nottingham, Seoul and New York.

www.behance.com/youvichow3b04
P206-207

YUKI INENAGA

YUKI graduated from the design school in 2017 and is currently working individually in Japan.

www.behance.net/yukiinenaga
P047

Yu-Min Tsai, Ann-Kristin Fuchs, Heiwa Wong

Yu-Min Tsai, Ann-Kristin Fuchs and Heiwa Wong are fellow students at Köln International School of Design in Cologne, Germany. Because of their similar tastes and styles in graphic design, they decided to team up for a self-initiated project about Risograph printing. This just might be the beginning and there is more to expect from the team.

www.behance.net/ymtsai
www.behance.net/ann-kristinfuchs
www.behance.net/heiwawong
P160-161

Acknowledgements

We would like to thank all of the designers involved for granting us permission to publish their works, as well as all of the photographers who have generously allowed us to use their images. We are also very grateful to many other people whose names do not appear in the credits but who made specific contributions and provided support. Without these people, we would not have been able to share these beautiful works with readers around the world. Our editorial team includes editor Desiree Wang and book designer Yingqiao Chen, to whom we are truly grateful.